CONTENTS

1.1 Africa in About 1600

Africa is a vast continent, more than three times the size of the USA and 120 times the size of the United Kingdom. One third of the land in Africa is **desert** and much of the remainder is very poor quality soil.

Over the thousands of years of African history, many different societies evolved. Over a thousand different languages were spoken. In some areas communities did not join together as states even though people spoke the same language and had similar cultures. Each town or village ran its own affairs. The **elders**, almost always the eldest men, made decisions. Women could discuss things but they were not allowed to make decisions.

Elsewhere **kingdoms** grew up with a centralized government. You have probably learned about Egypt, which was a kingdom 5,000 years ago. Egypt was ruled by a king called a **pharaoh** who had great power. In other parts of Africa similar states developed. Sometimes the kings conquered neighboring peoples and extended their kingdoms into **empires**.

B

The king of Ghana is a great king. In his territory are mines of gold, and under him a number of kingdoms, among them the kingdom of Sugham and the kingdom of Sama. In all this country there is gold.

The king of Ghana described by Al Yakubi, a ninth century Arab writer.

C

This city is great, flourishing and prosperous. Here gather the merchants who bring salt from the mines of Teghaza and those who bring gold from the mines of Bitou. It is because of this fortunate city that the caravans flock to Timbuktu from all points of the horizon.

Djenné is surrounded by a rampart that used to have eleven gates, but three have been walled up. God has drawn to this fortunate city a number of men, strangers to the country, who have come to live here.

A description of the city of Djenné, on the River Niger, by Es-Sa'di, a civil servant in Djenné. He was born in Timbuktu in 1596.

A

Mansa Musa, the man in the center of this map, was the Emperor of Mali in the early 14th century. He was known all over North and West Africa as a great emperor and devout Muslim.

Kings ruled from capital cities. Kingdoms often had other towns as well. Most houses in towns and cities were made from mud-bricks or woven sticks covered with mud (wattle and daub). In cities families usually lived in a single house. In villages families lived in a fenced compound with separate buildings for the husband, wife (or wives) and sons growing into manhood. Other buildings were used for storing grain or sheltering animals.

Large towns were centers of trade or manufacturing. Among themselves Africans traded goods such as ironware, pottery, cloth, vegetables, grain, spices and basketwork. They either exchanged their products or used things like cowrie shells as money. Africans also traded with people from abroad. Gold, leather, ivory, iron and copper were exchanged for fine European cloth, horses from Arab lands, Indian cotton, porcelain and glass from China and Persia (now called Iran).

There were many religions in Africa. By the 16th century there were Christians in Egypt, Ethiopia and places along the East Coast. Islam had spread across North Africa, across the northern parts of the West African kingdoms and to the East Coast. Islam brought the Arabic language to many places. Most people in West and Southern Africa had their own forms of religion; they believed in some form of 'Supreme Being' or god, and respect for ancestors. They also believed that there were good and evil spirits in the everyday things that surrounded them.

In some areas, climate and terrain made trade and agriculture difficult. Until camels and horses were imported there were no working animals to carry goods. Disease spread by the tse-tse fly killed off cattle in hot, damp areas. Nevertheless, most African people grew enough to feed themselves and to sell at market.

Mansa Musa

Mansa Kankan Musa (died about 1337) was a great emperor in West Africa. He built the Jingereber mosque in Timbuktu. In 1324 he went on a pilgrimage to Mecca. He took 8,000 men with him, including 500 slaves. Each slave carried a staff of pure gold. He visited Cairo, where he was treated with great honor by the Sultan of Egypt. While there, Mansa Musa was so generous with his gold that it caused a long term collapse in the value of Egyptian money.

The words we use, especially names, often also show how we feel about the people or things that are being described. In the text of this book we usually talk about Black peoples to describe peoples of African descent. In the sources we have kept the words used at the time. Often these words were intended to hurt or degrade people. They can tell us something about the ideas of the people who used them.

A mosque in Djenné, in Mali. Mali was an important kingdom in the 16th century.

D

SOURCE

1.2 The Empire of Songhai

Expansion of the empire of Songhai

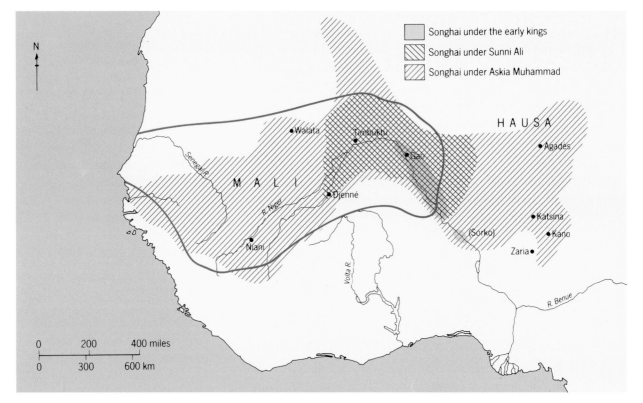

There were many African kingdoms. We shall look at just one of them, **Songhai**.

Songhai became rich from the trade routes across the Sahara desert. In the 11th century it started to expand. In 1330 Songhai was conquered by the Emperor of Mali, but King Sonni Ali threw him out in 1375 and began to extend the kingdom. By the time he died in 1492, King Sonni Ali had conquered all the neighboring countries to the north and west, including the cities of Djenné, Walata and Timbuktu. Sonni Ali's son became king, but he was overthrown by a general, Muhammad Turé, who gave himself the title **Askia** (Emperor).

Askia Muhammad was a wise ruler. He divided his empire into four regions, each ruled by a **viceroy**. The regions were further divided into provinces, run by **governors**. There were judges, tax collectors and market inspectors in each province and city. Taxes, especially on the gold trade, were collected regularly and fairly with no illegal demands. Taxes were paid in gold and goods. There were also special royal farms to produce food for trade.

A SOURCE

The people of Walata were generous and entertained me. They obtain water from the ground. Mutton is obtainable in quantity there. The clothes of its people are of fine Egyptian material. The women are extremely beautiful and are more important than the men. Gao is one of the finest towns in the Negrolands, with rice in plenty, milk and fish, and there is a type of cucumber which has no equal.

From 'The Travels of Ibn Battuta' written in the 14th century. He was a Berber, born in Tangier, who traveled the Muslim world from West Africa to India and China.

Askia Muhammad's capital city was **Gao**. There he had ministries for **justice**, **finance**, **defense** and **agriculture**. To help trade he made all merchants use standard weights and measures and had the highways guarded so that they were safe for travelers. Djenné, Walata and Timbuktu became centers of learning and Muslim religious teaching. In Timbuktu alone there were 150 schools and a university.

Askia Muhammad was a very religious man. In 1497, he went on a pilgrimage to the holy city of Mecca in Arabia. He gave ten thousand gold coins to help the poor and to build a hostel where pilgrims from West Africa could stay. The **Sharif** of Mecca, the head of the Muslim faith, gave Askia Muhammad the title of **Kalif** (religious ruler) of West Africa.

When Askia Muhammad returned to Songhai he extended his Empire by conquering all the lands that had once belonged to the Empire of Mali. He also took some of the land of the Hausa nation to the east. However, by 1528 Askia Muhammad was old and blind. He was overthrown by his son Musa.

The Songhai empire was later conquered by the Sultan (king) of Morocco, Mulay Ahmed el-Mansur. Despite enormous losses crossing the Sahara in 1589, the Moroccans defeated the Songhai. The Moroccan army had guns and small cannon. The Songhai army were armed only with spears, arrows and swords. The Moroccans looted the cities of Timbuktu and Gao and stayed until 1618.

From 'A History and Description of Africa' by Hassan ibn Mohammed, a Spanish-born Moor and great scholar, written about 1526.

Ibn Battuta

Muhammed ibn Abdullah ibn Battuta (1304–about 1377) was the most traveled of all the Muslim writers of the Middle Ages. He spent most of his life traveling. His writings give us a unique picture of 14th century Africa. He crossed the western Sahara and visited Walata, where he was shocked by the manners of the women. Nevertheless he remained for 50 days before continuing on to other cities and the court of Mali. He met rulers and dignitaries, reporting events with humor and accuracy.

B

SOURCE

The Sankore mosque in Timbuktu, built in the early 14th century. The mosque has never needed to be rebuilt because it has been continuously repaired.

1.3 Africa and the Rest of the World

Merchants from Europe and Asia traded with Africans for products such as iron, copper, ivory and gold. African people also traveled to many parts of the world. There were settlements of Africans on the west coast of India. African slave-soldiers were in the armies of several Indian states. Some Africans became governors, officials and rulers of states where they had settled.

There is evidence that some Africans went to China, probably to trade. They may have crossed the Atlantic before Columbus. African slaves and free men fought in the Muslim armies in North Africa, Arabia and Europe. Some of these slaves became important people. Women slaves from Africa were sold into the **harems** of rich Arabs and Ottomans.

One Muslim army, comprising Arabs and North and West Africans, began conquering the countries we now call Spain and Portugal in AD 710. These invaders, called 'Moors' by Europeans, ruled parts of these countries for over 700 years. During this time learning was encouraged, medicine and science progressed, and the arts flourished. There was religious freedom. Women were allowed to take up professions and some became historians, philosophers, surgeons and doctors.

Africa and its contacts with the rest of the world

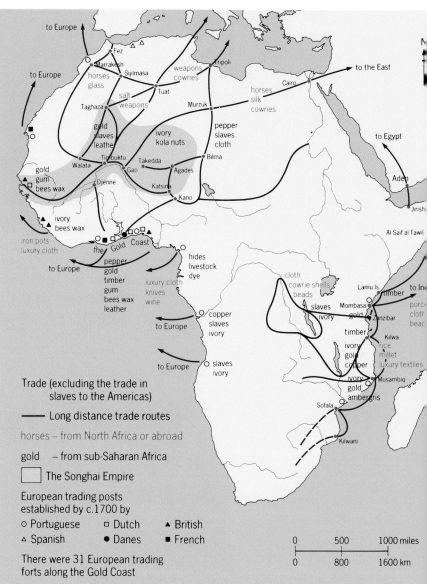

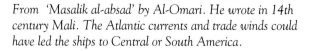

A

SOURCE

The captain replied, 'Sultan, we sailed for a long while until we met with a strong current flowing in the open sea. The others sailed on but did not come back.'

From 'Masalik al-absad' by Al-Omari. He wrote in 14th century Mali. The Atlantic currents and trade winds could have led the ships to Central or South America.

A portrait of Malik Ambar. He was sold as a slave to an Arab judge. Malik became ruler of Ahmadnagar in India 1607–26.

Abu'l-Hasan

Abu'l-Hasan (789–857) was the most famous musician and poet in Cordova, a part of al-Andalus, Moorish Spain. Abu'l-Hasan lived in the reigns of al-Hakam I and Abd al-Rahman II. These rulers are said to have given him a luxurious mansion and to have paid him 3,280 dinars per month, with large bonuses to perform at religious festivals. He was known as 'Zinyab' ('a bird with black feathers') because his skin was so dark. Abu'l-Hasan was a remarkable man who introduced the guitar to Europe and also invented a pleasant tasting toothpaste. He was born a slave, but he died a wealthy and honored man.

In the 15th century, European countries wanted to expand their trade and cut out the Arab, Indian and African traders. Explorers set out to find new trade routes. The Portuguese Bartholomew Diaz and Vasco da Gama sailed down the West African coast, round the Cape of Good Hope, up the east coast and across to India. By the end of the 17th century, Spain, Portugal, Holland, France, Denmark, Sweden and England had set up trading posts along the African coastline.

One of a number of eight foot high heads found in a religious center in Mexico dating from about AD 500.

1.4 The Americas in About 1600

In 1600 the Americas – North, Central and South – were populated by Native Americans, Europeans and Africans. The **Native Americans** (sometimes called North American Indians) lived in many different groups and spoke hundreds of different languages.

In **North America** there were five main groups. The **Inuits**, or Eskimos, lived in small hunting and fishing groups in the far north. In the coastal forests, the **North East** and **North West people** were farmers, hunters and fishermen, skilled at crafts.

A **SOURCE**

These people are very numerous and of good appearance. Our men found them very pleasant and were well received.

Christopher Columbus, talking about Native Americans in 1498.

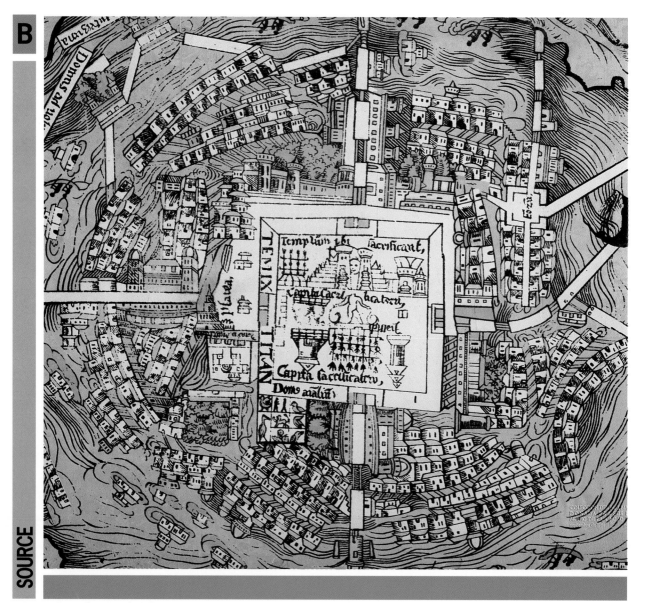

B **SOURCE**

Mexico City, the capital of the Aztec Empire, as the Spanish found it when they arrived in Central America.

The **Pueblo** peoples of the dry South West lived in villages, raising corn and livestock. They had councils chosen by priests. Women owned all the property and controlled the distribution of food.

The **Plains Indians** such as the Sioux, Cheyennes and Comanches were people who originally settled in one place. They were driven onto the plains by Europeans. They acquired horses from the Spaniards and lived nomadically, following the herds of buffalo they hunted.

In the **Caribbean Islands** there were three main groups of people – Taino, Arawaks and Caribs. Little is known about them as almost all were killed by the Europeans.

In **South and Central America** the empires and cities of the Incas and Aztecs were totally destroyed by the Europeans. Gold, silver and books were seized by the Spanish. Around 30 million people were killed or died of European diseases.

The **Europeans** went to the Americas to search for gold and silver. They had guns and cannon, and took horses and donkeys for transport. They conquered the Caribbean Islands and all of South and Central America. The first were the Spanish. They were followed by the French, who settled in north east North America and the Caribbean. Landless English poor and people like Puritans and Quakers, fleeing from religious persecution, settled in colonies on the east coast of North America.

Some Africans were taken to North America by the Europeans, but until 1660 few were slaves. Most were like **indentured servants** – who sold themselves to an employer for a fixed period of time. In South and Central America, however, by 1640 the Spanish and the Portuguese had imported over a half a million enslaved Africans. Other Europeans soon took up this idea; many thousands of Africans were taken to the Americas to work on plantations and in mines. African slaves were treated as **chattel** slaves which meant that they had no more rights than a horse or a chair!

Native Americans having their hands cut off for failing to give the Spanish enough gold. The picture is from 'Historia de las Indias' by Bartolome de las Casas, about 1550. De las Casas was a Spanish priest who lived in the Spanish colonies for many years. The Spanish colonizers forced Native Americans to work for them.

Estevanico

Estevanico (about 1500–39) was an African who went to the Americas with Cortez. Estevanico explored Mexico, Arizona and Florida, where in 1528 he and his companions were captured by Native Americans. They escaped, but did not reach a safe Spanish settlement for eight years.

Estevanico was later asked to guide an expedition to the fabled 'Seven Cities of Gold'. In 1539 this expedition approached the territory of the Zuni people. The Zuni attacked them and Estevanico was killed.

2.1 The Slave Trade

When Europeans first began to settle in the Americas they used **indentured** laborers to work farms and mines. But there were few indentured servants due to the wars in Europe in the 17th and 18th centuries. Also, they only worked for seven years before their contracts were fulfilled and they were free again. Because of these problems and their desire to make a lot of money, Europeans began to enslave Africans. Africa was the only part of the 'known' world that was not controlled by rulers who had weapons as powerful as those of the Europeans. So, from about 1510, the Spaniards and Portuguese began to capture Africans and ship them to the Americas. By 1570 there were about 20,000 African slaves in Mexico, mainly working in silver mines.

The first slave traders went to the western coast of Africa. They exchanged their horses, guns and alcohol for food, ivory, gold and slaves. Later the Europeans wanted *only* slaves.

A

SOURCE

We saw slaves of both sexes chained together. Many were mere skeletons. In some the chains had, by their constant action, worn through the flesh to the bare bone. The ulcerated wound had become the home for thousands of flies which had laid their eggs in the cavities.

Commodore Owen, a British naval officer, describing the condition of slaves in a Portugese trade fort in 1825.

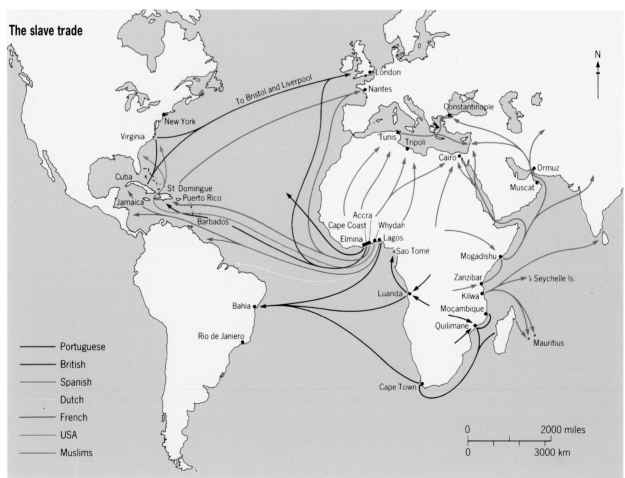

The slave trade

- Portuguese
- British
- Spanish
- Dutch
- French
- USA
- Muslims

0   2000 miles
0   3000 km

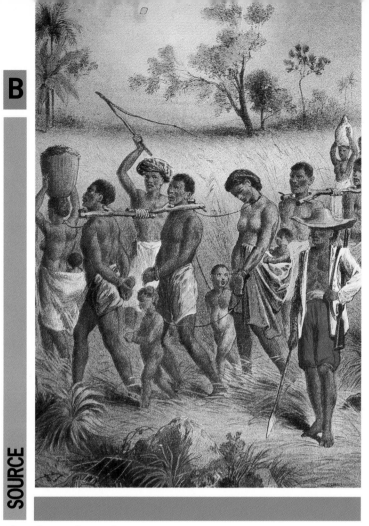

Slaves being taken to the coast for transportation.

Because of the great demand, the trade in slaves was very profitable. Many European nations joined in. They built forts along the West African coast which were heavily defended against other Europeans. Inside the forts the slaves were held in **barracoons**, which were overcrowded, dark and airless prisons, often at least partly underground. Because of these terrible conditions many of the captives died in the weeks or months that they had to wait for the arrival of the **slavers**. Slavers were sailing ships that were specially fitted out to carry the slaves away from Africa.

Using their new guns, coastal Africans began to raid their neighbors inland. Men, women and children were captured and marched to the coast to be sold to the Europeans. Many died on the journey.

It is difficult to know how many Africans were captured and how many of them reached the Americas. One fairly conservative estimate is that between 1490 and 1890 over six million women and nine million men were taken from Africa. It is thought that an equal number died before they could be exported.

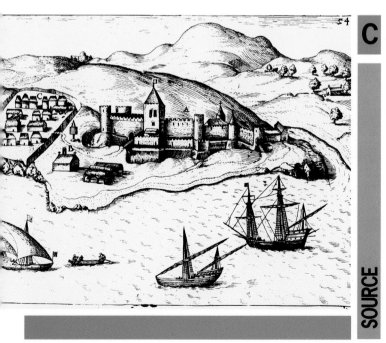

The Castle of Mina

Hawkins

Sir John Hawkins (1532–95) became the first Englishman to traffic in slaves in 1562. He captured Black West Africans, and took them to the Spanish West Indies. His slave trading ended in 1567 when he was beaten by Spaniards.

2.2 Effects of the Slave Trade on Africa

The slave trade across the Atlantic Ocean changed the whole course of African history. The kings and chiefs of the African coastal communities became trading partners with the European merchants who had set up business there. They swapped men, women and children for European goods. Eventually, many of the traders were of mixed race with European fathers and African mothers. These **go-betweens** were in positions of power and influence.

Kings who had once protected their people now became warmongers and kidnappers. They invented crimes for which the punishment was being sold as a slave. Some, when drunk with European alcohol, sold their own people. Prisoners captured in wars were sold as slaves, so the Europeans interfered and provoked wars between African kingdoms.

As the demand for slaves grew, raiding and kidnapping spread terror deep into Africa. Continuous warfare, raiding parties and killings led to famine. Fear and insecurity spread over the land. Frightened villagers, trying to escape the raiders, moved into remote areas which often had poor soil which produced few crops.

B SOURCE

At Bonny, on the Niger delta, slaves are purchased of the king, who is the principal trader.

Evidence of Liverpool trader James Penny to Parliament, 1789.

C SOURCE

The Europeans did not introduce manufacturing plants, agricultural methods, political systems or Christian ideals. What they introduced were muskets, gunpowder and rum, all as a means of advancing the slave trade. In 1853 a British official wrote 'It may be safely affirmed that from our first settlement on the coast to the abolition of the slave trade in 1807, we did not confer one lasting benefit upon the people.'

From 'Black Cargoes' by D. P. Mannix and M. Cowley, 1962.

A SOURCE

Slaves abandoned by traders because they were too weak to continue the march to the coast. These slaves were being taken to Arabia, a trade which was still in existence at the beginning of this century. A drawing from the published diaries of the explorer David Livingstone, 1874.

The Oba (king) of Benin also tried to resist the trade in slaves. From Dapper, 'Description of Africa', 1688. Dapper was a Dutch geographer.

The ancient overland trade routes were abandoned in favor of coastal trading stations. People along the old routes lost their income and livelihood. African trade in other products declined as huge quantities of European goods flooded the continent.

Some African peoples tried to defend themselves and to fight back. For example the small kingdom of Dahomey was often raided by the slave traders of the kingdom of Oyo. King Agaja II (1708–32) wanted to stop this. He even sent a message of protest to the King of Britain. He built up a strong army which included all the young men and women. But the Oyo king had guns and King Agaja only had spears. The Dahomeans could only get guns from the European traders in exchange for people who were then sold as slaves. To protect themselves the Dahomeans had to become slave catchers.

The King of Dahomey leading men and women soldiers, from a book published in Britain in 1793, by Archibald Denzer, a supporter of slavery.

The Africans became the architects of their own ruin. The most lucrative occupation became war to get slaves. It was only then that permanent insecurity, endless raids and the misery and famine that come with them, became permanent features of Black Africa.

From 'Senegalese Kingdoms' by C. Becker and V. Martin, 1982.

Tomba

Tomba was thus described in 1735: 'I could not help noticing among them a tall fellow of strong make and bold, stern aspect. He seemed to disdain his fellow slaves for their readiness to be chained. He scorned looking at us, refusing to stretch out his limbs as his master commanded. This got him an unmerciful beating which the Negro bore calmly.'

Tomba was a Baga chief, the leader of some country villages in West Africa who resisted the attacks of slave traders. The traders together surprised and overcame Tomba. On board the ship *Robert* of Bristol, Tomba and others decided to kill the ship's company and escape. They almost succeeded, but they were captured and tortured. Tomba was too valuable to kill but the rest were 'sentenced to cruel deaths, making them first eat the heart and liver of one of them killed'.

2.3 The Middle Passage

As the number of European settlers in the American colonies increased, a triangular trade developed between Europe, Africa and the Americas. Ships with European goods sailed to Africa. The goods were exchanged for human beings. The enslaved Africans were taken to the Americas and sold to the settlers. With the profits the slaver captain bought colonial produce like sugar, rum, cotton and tobacco. He then sailed back to Europe and sold the cargo for another handsome profit. The crossing from Africa to the Americas was called the **Middle Passage**.

One man, Olaudah Equiano, who was captured and sold at the age of eleven, wrote down his experience of the Middle Passage. Sources B and D show us what it was like.

Conditions on the Middle Passage were so cruel that some slaves committed suicide to escape their misery. In a few cases the slaves mutinied: they took over the ship and made their escape.

Olaudah Equiano.

I was soon put under the decks where, with the stench and my grief, I became so sick that I was unable to eat. For not eating I was beaten. I would have jumped over the side of the ship but I could not. The crew watched us closely. The stench of the hold, the heat and the crowding, which meant that each had scarcely room to turn himself, almost suffocated us. There was sickness among the slaves of which many died. The situation was aggravated by the rubbing of the chains and the filth of the lavatory-buckets into which the children often fell. The shrieks of the women and the groans of the dying rendered the whole a scene of horror.

I became so sick that, as I was a young boy, my chains were removed and I was allowed to stay on deck. One day, two of my wearied countrymen who were chained together, preferring death to such a life of misery, jumped into the sea.

From 'The Interesting Narrative of the Life of Olaudah Equiano' by himself, 1789. Equiano bought his freedom and settled in Britain. He became an anti-slavery campaigner.

Currency

Some money in this book is listed in British sterling (pounds). The **rate of exchange** fluctuates and in 1994 is about $1.65 for every £1.00. When the dollar was created as the USA standard currency in the 1700s, the pound was worth five dollars.

The **buying power** of the dollar ($) and the pound (£) in the 1700s was about 50 times what it is today. So when you read on page 17 that **Olaudah Equiano** saved £140, think of it as nearly $12,000 in today's money!

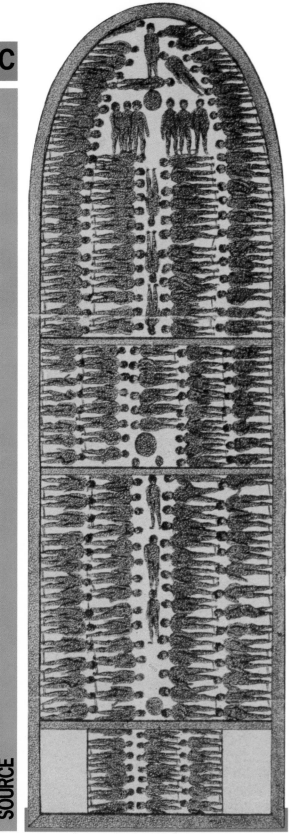

A plan of how slaves were packed into a ship, from a book written in 1834 by Thomas Clarkson, an anti-slavery campaigner.

D

At last we anchored off Bridgetown (in Barbados). Many merchants and planters (plantation owners) came on board and examined us attentively. They also made us jump. We were penned up like so many sheep. We were sold. In this manner, without scruple, relations and friends were separated, most of them never to see each other again. I and some few more slaves that were not saleable were shipped off to Virginia, where I was sold to a planter. I was exceedingly miserable as I had no person to speak to that I could understand. I was horrified to see in the kitchens a Black woman slave who was cruelly loaded with various kinds of iron machines. She had one particularly on her head which locked her mouth so fast that she could scarcely speak and could not eat nor drink.

From 'The Interesting Narrative of the Life of Olaudah Equiano' by himself, 1789.

E

The violence of the Africans, by murdering whole crews and destroying ships when they can, calls for the same confinements as if they were wolves or wild boars.

From 'History of Jamaica' by E. Long, 1774.

Equiano

Olaudah Equiano (1745–97) was born in what is today Nigeria. He and his sister were captured and taken to the West Indies. He was eventually sold to a Quaker, Robert King of Philadelphia, who allowed him to trade on his own behalf. Equiano made enough money to buy his own freedom for £140. This was a low price for a man who could read, write, calculate and navigate. He was 21 years old. Equiano went to Britain and worked as a sailor, where he was very active in abolitionist circles. He wrote a fascinating autobiography, still available today.

2.4 Slave-worked Economies

There were African slaves in America very soon after the arrival of the first Europeans. Enslaved Africans accompanied the Spanish conquistadores (the soldiers who conquered Central and South America). Very soon the economies of most of the European colonies became dependent on slave labor.

In **South and Central America** the Spanish and Portuguese settlers at first used only a few slaves as domestic servants and farm workers. As the European demand for sugar increased, more slaves were imported from the Congo and Angola regions of West Africa.

In Mexico and Peru slaves worked in silver-ore crushing mills. They mined copper in Cuba, Venezuela and Brazil; gold on the Pacific coast and diamonds in Brazil. As cities like Lima and Rio de Janeiro grew, slaves performed domestic service and worked as trades and craftworkers. They also worked on farms growing food for local use.

Although the Spanish built large towns in the **Caribbean Islands**, the vast majority of slaves worked on plantations growing cotton, tobacco, indigo and, later, sugar. There were a few craftworkers on all the plantations and domestic servants in the plantation owners' houses and in towns.

A **SOURCE**

I suppose nine-tenths of the mechanics throughout the West Indies are Negro slaves. I well know the coopers among them earn two dollars a day, the carpenters the same and oftentimes more.

From 'The Interesting Narrative of the Life of Olaudah Equiano' by himself, 1789.

B **SOURCE**

Slaves washing for diamonds in Brazil.

Cotton from slave-worked plantations awaiting shipment from New Orleans. Lithograph by Currier and Ives, 1884.

In the Northern States of North America settlements and farms were small. Some European families used enslaved Africans as household servants and as craftsworkers such as carpenters, stonemasons, barrel makers, carriage makers, blacksmiths and weavers. Some owners hired out skilled slaves by the day. Others set up slave-staffed shops such as tailors, shoemakers and watchmakers. Slaves also worked in the forests, cutting timber and making charcoal. On the coast slaves worked in shipping as shipwrights, sailmakers and sailors. Slavery was not widespread in the Northern States. The number of slaves there was small compared with the Southern States, South America and the Caribbean.

Slaves in the Southern States worked in the same kind of jobs as in the North. They also labored on farms growing rice, tobacco, coffee and cotton for export. After 1793 technology for processing cotton improved. More cotton was exported, so slaves were made to work harder than ever. In 1850, an estimated 1,815,000 slaves were engaged in producing cotton. Slaves were also employed in rice and sugar production and saw mills. They were fishermen (there were 20,000 in 1860), coal and iron miners and roadbuilders. Each state received a large income by making owners pay a tax on every slave they bought.

The slave may be 'used up' in seven years – used as a 'breeder', as a prostitute, to serve drink and as a subject of surgical experiments – but the law says that he may not be used as a clerk.

William Goodell commenting on the American state slave laws, in 'American Slavery: a Formidable Obstacle to the Conversion of the World', 1854.

Bradley

Benjamin Bradley (born 1835) was born a slave. He was hired out to work in a printing office, where he showed great skills. Using bits of scrap materials, he built a working steam engine model. His master saw his talents and moved him to the Naval Academy at Annapolis as a laboratory assistant. Bradley's master let him keep $5 a month from his wages, from which he saved enough to build a full size engine that could drive a warship. Friends lent Bradley $1,000 to buy his freedom, which he paid back quickly.

2.5 Conditions Under Slavery

At the beginning of European settlement, African slaves and European indentured servants worked together. Over the years the number of new indentured servants declined. The settlers wanted more labor to provide for their needs and to grow export crops. The numbers of imported African slaves grew rapidly and their lives got worse. In the Caribbean there were more slaves than Europeans. The planters were afraid of rebellion. They followed a policy of control through fear.

Slaves had no rights. They were seen as possessions, rather than human beings. They were not paid wages. Owners could deal with slaves exactly as they pleased, and planters enforced the laws. There was no punishment for owners who worked their slaves to death. Until the 19th century, no one questioned owners burning or torturing their slaves. If a European murdered another man's slave he had only to pay a fine for destroying property! However, until 1750, if a slave killed a European, he was put to death by slow torture.

Slaves were not allowed to –
- legally marry
- own property
- inherit or bequeath property
- give evidence in court against a European
- read or write

Slaves could not –
- prevent their children being sold
- protect their families from their owner's brutality
- usually be granted or buy their own freedom

Slaves had to –
- do whatever work their owners ordered
- work whatever hours the owner demanded
- accept any European man's sexual advances

A

SOURCE

Branding a female slave on the west coast of Africa, from 'Captain Canot, or Twenty Years of an African Slaver', 1853.

Richmond slave market in the early 19th century. Most slaves were bought and sold at degrading auctions like this.

Slave laws varied in harshness from state to state. Some of them changed slowly, for a variety of reasons.

- Some Europeans who had fathered children born to slave mothers wanted to free their children, to educate them and to leave them property.
- Some churchmen, missionaries, liberal owners and governors forced some improvements.
- As the price of slaves went up, owners wanted to extend the slaves' working lives rather than work them to death.
- Whites, especially in the Caribbean, grew to rely on things such as vegetables, fish, pottery and baskets that the slaves produced in their free time.

Although there were some improvements, after a rebellion laws were usually made more harsh.

C

SOURCE

I beg to state that the feeding and the nature of labor of the slaves in these islands has been notorious for many years.

Governor Maxwell of St. Kitts, 1832, reporting on conditions to the British government.

D

SOURCE

Coffey

Alvin Coffey was taken by his master to California to mine for gold in 1849. He was allowed to work for himself at night, and saved $700. Then his master took his money and sold him. Coffey's new, honest owner also allowed him to do his own work after finishing his tasks. Coffey bought freedom for his family and himself. They became one of the first farming families in Tahoma County, California.

A Birmingham Anti-Slavery Society poster.

2.6 Enslaved Africans

As the centuries passed, new arrivals to the colonies from both Europe and Africa were absorbed into well developed societies. Each level of society had its own social structure, religion, language and culture. The top level of society was the Europeans. Next came the free people of African descent, then the slaves of mixed race and finally slaves of unmixed African descent. In North America, the most important distinction in society was between Whites and non-Whites.

There were also levels in slave societies. Highly skilled slaves, some of whom could earn some money for themselves, were the highest level. On plantations, the **drivers** were on the top (these were the slaves who drove the pace of work with a whip). The drivers were often of mixed race. Next came those with special skills and domestic servants. Finally there were the field laborers.

Some owners encouraged **creole** slaves (those born in the colony) to feel superior to newly arrived Africans. Owners hoped that creating divisions between slaves would prevent them joining together in rebellion. They also reinforced the idea of color superiority.

The Roman Catholic Spanish and Portuguese colonists baptized slaves but did not teach them Christian ideals. In the Caribbean Protestant colonies, Christian religious teaching was denied to slaves until about 1800. Slaves developed their own religions, based on African beliefs. They believed that their priests, male and female, had the power to control good and evil. These religions were often banned by owners who said that the priests preached disobedience and revolt.

A **SOURCE**

Their music consisted of nothing but Gambys (Eboe drums), Shaky–shekies and Kitty–katties. The latter is any flat board beaten with two sticks, and the former is a bladder with pebbles in it. But the main part of the music to which they dance is vocal. One girl singing two lines by herself is answered by a chorus.

Description of Black music by Matthew Lewis, a plantation and slave owner, in 1834.

Slaves dancing on the French-owned island of Dominica around 1810.

B **SOURCE**

Africans had their own music. They made drums and stringed instruments and sang in the African 'call and response' style. African dances and music were eventually mixed with European styles.

In some areas owners provided housing for their slaves, in others slaves built their own homes. At first these were like the houses from their part of Africa. All had thatched roofs. Thatching was a prized skill among slaves, as were the weaving of matting, basketmaking, carpentry and pottery.

The slaves spoke many different languages. They had to develop a language with which to talk to each other and to their owners. These new languages, called **creoles**, used both African and European words and African grammar. Today there are French, English and Spanish creoles.

What enslaved Africans could not recreate was African family structure. Slaves could not legally marry each other. Living together was not secure, as slaves could be sold at any time. In Spanish and Portuguese colonies African women lived openly with white men, but they rarely married. These relationships were just as common in Protestant areas, like the English and Dutch colonies, but they were usually kept secret.

Slavery was inherited from the mother, so children with White fathers and slave mothers were slaves. Children were taken from their mothers soon after birth. Women often aborted their pregnancies or killed their babies to prevent children being born into slavery. Margaret Garner was a slave who killed two of her children rather than have them made slaves. She committed suicide when her other children were taken.

Slaves formed new kinds of relationships – **shipmates** and **godparents**. Shipmates were people who had shared the horrors of the Middle Passage. Godparents were either Christian godparents or a respected slave adopted by a younger slave.

Craft

Ellen Craft (1827–97) was born a slave in Georgia. Her father was the slave owner to whom her mother belonged. When Ellen was eleven years old she was given as a wedding present to her father's legal daughter – her half sister. At her new home, she fell in love with another slave, William Craft. They did not want to marry and have children who would be born as slaves. They were able to escape and ran away to safety in England.

3.1 The West Indian Colonies

A map of Caribbean colonies, around 1815.

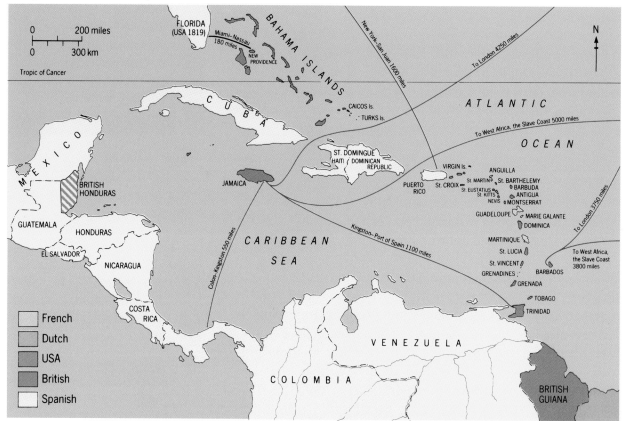

Throughout the 17th and 18th centuries Europeans waged war against each other in Europe and the Americas. European possessions in the Caribbean changed hands many times. The British government set up elected Assemblies in its colonies. Only very rich Whites could stand for election and only wealthy Europeans could vote. The Governor, sent from Britain, was in charge. Laws had to be approved by the British Parliament; this included the cruel slave laws.

At first, the Assemblies did not make laws about slaves. As they were considered to be property, like horses or carts, they came under laws that covered property. Later, fear of rebellions caused harsh laws to be passed to control all aspects of slaves' lives. Slaves still had no rights.

In most colonies only one crop was grown – sugar, nutmeg or cotton. These were exported to Britain where any surplus was re-exported. Slaves did almost all the work, much of it by hand. They were cheaper to import than machinery.

A None of the evils of slavery are more horrible than the treatment of females. They were obliged to submit to prostitution, to equal labor with males and to become breeders of slaves at the will and pleasure of the master.

SOURCE

From the 'Journal' of Major J. B. Colthurst, a special magistrate sent from Britain to the Caribbean, published in 1847.

To feed their slaves some planters imported food, mainly from North America. Clothing and equipment for sugar processing were imported from Britain. So when Britain was at war there were shortages and hunger in the colonies. In colonies with plenty of land, the planters gave slaves bits of the land that were unsuitable for the export crop. The slaves grew food for themselves on these 'provision grounds'. They could sell any surplus at local markets.

Slaves outnumbered Whites by about eight to one in the colonies. In 1807 there were about 652,000 slaves on British owned islands, far fewer than had been imported. More men than women slaves were imported. Conditions were so bad that few babies were born to slaves and even fewer survived.

Another group in the population was the **mulattoes**. They were mixed-race people, usually with slave mothers and European fathers. Sometimes they were freed by their fathers but they still did not have the same rights as Whites.

SOURCE B

Everyone seems keen to make money and no one cares about how it is made. The Europeans are lazy and think of nothing but eating, drinking and enjoying themselves. They consider the Negroes as creatures merely formed for their comfort and to do their orders.

From the 'Journal' of Lady Nugent, wife of the Governor of Jamaica, 1801–5.

Williams

Francis Williams (born about 1700) was born in Jamaica, the third son of a free African couple. Because he showed great intelligence, the Governor, the Duke of Montague, decided to send him to England to be educated. He went to grammar school and then to Cambridge University where he studied classics and mathematics.

When he passed his exams, the Duke tried to get him appointed to the island Council. Trelawney, the new Governor, objected, so the Duke helped Williams set up a school in Spanish Town. Both African and European children went to his school to learn Latin, reading, mathematics and writing. Williams became so well respected that James Ramsay, an abolitionist who visited Jamaica, could say that, 'gentlemen of Jamaica speak highly of Francis Williams'.

▼ *A 'driver' whipping a slave, 1843.*

SOURCE C

3.2 The West Indies: Resistance

Slaves hated the way they were treated. They were not paid for their work so they saw no reason for working hard. They sabotaged their owners by working slowly and inefficiently. They broke tools and let animals loose. Wheels mysteriously came off carriages, horses became lame, expensive clothes were ruined in the wash and best china dishes fell off shelves. Owners rarely recognized this as resistance.

Slaves pretended to be ill. They played deaf and dumb, and couldn't understand English when they did not want to. They acted 'sassy' (cheeky) and were very clever at making fun of their owners. Some slaves even burned canefields and planters' homes, or poisoned their owners. They were harshly punished for such behavior. As well as the usual whipping, slaves had their ears, noses and limbs cut off. They were sometimes buried alive or had all their bones broken. For the most serious offenses slaves were killed.

Many slaves ran away. On some islands hiding was impossible so **runaways** stowed away on boats to Spanish colonies, which never returned runaways. In Cuba, foreign runaways were given their freedom if they were baptized into the Roman Catholic Church. Some runaways joined pirates. On mountainous islands like Jamaica runaways fled to the mountains. These people were called **Maroons** (after the Spanish word 'címarron' meaning 'wild'). Maroons lived in remote areas, growing their own food and raiding plantations for guns and anything else they needed.

Not all runaways stayed free. In Jamaica, captured runaways were held in the workhouse. If they were unclaimed they were sold. If they had been absent for over six months they were executed.

B **SOURCE**

Negro slaves understand better than anyone a species of annoyance which, though it has been impossible not to see that the act has been planned, can yet be passed off so well as a mistake, that you have not the power of giving them a reproof over it.

Mrs Carmichael, a British woman who lived in the West Indies between 1820 and 1832.

C **SOURCE**

A runaway slave being hung by the ribs, Surinam 1773. An engraving by Stedman.

A **SOURCE**

General Nugent received an express letter from Mr Henry of St Mary's parish with an account of several Negroes having suddenly disappeared, and that from his own place fifteen had gone off at once. God preserve us from an insurrection!

Written by Lady Nugent, wife of the Governor of Jamaica, in 1805.

SOURCE

A Jamaican Slave House of Correction. Runaways were taken here for punishment and to await being reclaimed by their owners.

E

SOURCE

1776: Jack, for being a runaway, sentenced to be immediately carried to the place of execution and there to be hanged by the neck until he is dead, and his head to be cut off in the most public place on the said estate.

1776: Adam, for running away, to be taken to the place from where he came, to have a halter put about his neck, and one of his ears nailed to a post, and that the executioner then causes the said ear to be cut off close to his head.

1783: Priscilla, for running away, both her ears cut off close to her head immediately, to receive 39 lashes the first Monday in every month for one year and to be worked in irons during that time.

Punishments listed in the Court Session book for the parish of St Thomas-in-the-East, Jamaica.

F

SOURCE

A surprising number of Negroes and mulattoes were listed among the pirate crews. Some were runaway slaves while others were free men. In some companies one sixth of the total numbers of pirates were Negro. Captured Negro pirates were usually hanged along with their white comrades, but occasionally they were sold into slavery.

From 'The Golden Age of Piracy' by H. F. Rankin, 1969.

Mackendal

Mackendal (died 1760) was a slave brought from Guinea in West Africa to St Domingue, where he worked as a field hand. There his master tortured him and he lost an arm in an accident. He escaped to the mountains where, with his command of language and his fearlessness, he became leader of a Maroon band.

He tried to get the Maroons to unite to drive the Europeans out of St Domingue. His plan was to poison the water in all the capital city houses and kill any Whites left. He visited plantations at night to persuade slaves to join him. He was captured and burned, betrayed by one of the slaves he wanted to free.

3.3 The West Indies

Revolts and Rebellions

Slaves sometimes organized huge rebellions. Between 1635 and 1834 there were 41 rebellions in the British Caribbean Islands.

In Jamaica there were so many Maroons (escaped slaves) that they prevented the expansion of plantations into uncultivated areas. From 1729 the local militia attacked the Maroons but they could not conquer them. The Jamaica Assembly asked the British government for help. The war dragged on for 10 years until the Assembly offered the Maroons their freedom and an area of land in exchange for peace and the promise to return runaway slaves. The Maroons accepted. Two of the Maroon leaders, Cudjoe and Nanny, a woman believed to have magic powers, are popular heroes in Jamaica today.

B **SOURCE**

The Negroes permitted the sergeant and his party to pass unnoticed, but the minute us officers got under their ambush, a volley of shot came down and several of the soldiers were mortally wounded. The baggage Negroes ran away. All of the men in the militia, except their officer, followed. The wild Negroes at the same time were calling out 'Becara (White man) go away'.

From the memoirs of Philip Thicknesse, a British regular army officer on campaign against Maroons in 1739.

C

Very much shocked by an account of a massacre of 375 White persons in St Domingue. How dreadful!

From Lady Nugent's Journal, 22 November 1801.

A **SOURCE**

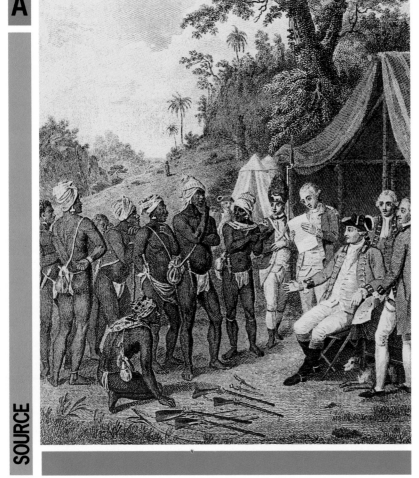

The British were forced to recognize the Maroons as free men.

Maroons also revolted on the French-held island of St Domingue. There were 3,000 rebels on St Domingue in 1751. They plotted to kill all the Whites but their leader, Mackendal, was betrayed, captured and burnt alive. In 1789 the French Revolution took place. The new government's slogan was **Liberté, Egalité, Fraternité** (Freedom, Equality, Brotherhood). It believed that slaves should be freed. The Whites and mixed-race **mulattoes** on St Domingue decided to ignore this and retained slavery. The slaves rose in revolt in 1791. The mulattoes fought the Whites as the Whites would not grant equality to the mixed-race people. The slaves fought both groups.

The planters asked the British for help. British forces, hoping to take St Domingue for themselves, invaded the island. They were defeated by the Black revolutionaries led by **Toussaint L'Ouverture**. By 1800 St Domingue was free from colonial rule. It was the only slave society overthrown by slave revolt.

Toussaint ruled a self-governing state within the French Empire. He renamed the country **Haiti**. In 1801 Napoleon Bonaparte, the new ruler of France, decided to reconquer Haiti and restore slavery. By treachery his troops captured Toussaint, but other leaders took over. Led by Jean-Jacques Dessalines, the Haitians defeated the French army in 1803. On 1 January 1804 Haiti declared total independence. Toussaint had however died in a French prison in 1803.

Toussaint L'Ouverture (1743–1803), first ruler of independent Haiti.

But what men these Blacks are! How they fight and how they die! Their reckless courage when they can no longer have recourse to stratagem! They advanced singing, for the Negro sings everywhere. Their song went as follows:

> To the attack, grenadier,
> Who gets killed, that's his affair,
> Forget your ma,
> Forget your pa,
> To the attack, grenadier,
> Who gets killed, that's his affair.

Lemmonier-Delafosse, an officer in Napoleon's army in St Domingue.

Down with Colonialism and Slavery – Haiti

The many years of war left a tradition of military rule. Another legacy of colonialism was racial tension between the mulattoes and the Blacks.

In 1804, Dessalines proclaimed himself Emperor of Haiti. He took the mulattoes' land and gave it to his favorite army officers. Although he was a military commander of genius, Dessalines was not a good administrator. There was tension in Haiti between Dessalines and his people. He could not restore productivity to the war damaged and neglected sugar plantations. The mulattoes rebelled. Haiti was split in two. Dessalines was assassinated.

Toussaint's general, Henri Christophe, succeeded Dessalines. He was elected president by the Black military leaders in 1806. In 1811 he was crowned King Henri I by the Archbishop of Haiti. Henri got sugar production going again and introduced just laws and schooling. But he was a tyrannical ruler. For example, it is said that 20,000 peasants died building his mountain-top fortress and that much of Haiti's small income was spent on his palace, Sans Souci.

The mulattoes fought against Henri and in 1820 the mass of the people rose in revolt. Already paralyzed by a stroke, Henri I shot himself. Haiti was reunited under the mulatto General Boyer. Racial tensions and violence continued. This allowed European companies to take over banking and commerce. By 1914 Haiti was bankrupt. The USA took control of the country and its finances and installed presidents of its choice.

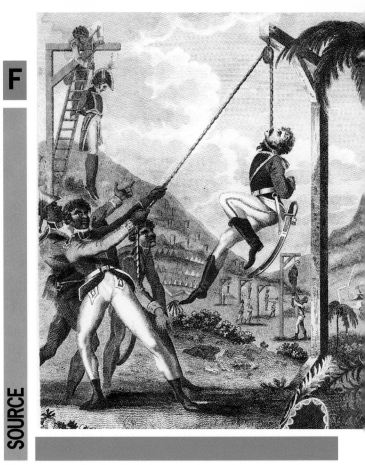

F SOURCE

'Revenge taken by the Black Army for the cruelties practised on them by the French', in Haiti, engraved by Barlow, 1805.

G SOURCE

Jean-Jacques Dessalines, liberator of Haiti.

One of his attendants, on hearing him lock his bedroom door, looked through the keyhole to see what was going on. He saw the king making himself comfortable in an armchair and immediately discharging one pistol through his head and another through his heart. He fell back and died before any alarm could be given.

A description of how King Henri Christophe of Haiti died in 1820.

Toussaint

François Dominique Toussaint (1743–1803) lived in St Domingue in 1789, when it was a wealthy French colony. In 1791 the slaves revolted when the planters refused to grant the liberty promoted by the French Revolutionary government. St Domingue was plunged into bloody chaos. The leader of one armed band was Toussaint, a 50 year old former slave who called himself 'L'Ouverture' because it was said he could find an opening through enemy lines anywhere.

When Britain and Spain invaded St Domingue, Toussaint became the military commander of the Republican forces. He appealed to all slaves – 'Brothers and Friends, I am Toussaint L'Ouverture. I have undertaken vengeance. I want liberty and equality to reign in St Domingue.' He defeated the British forces and forced them to evacuate the island.

In 1801, Toussaint drew up a constitution, and slavery was abolished. He was made Governor. This enraged Napoleon, who caused Toussaint to be overthrown and imprisoned in France, where he died.

Portrait of Henri Christophe, King of Haiti, painted by Richard Evans.

3.4 British Profits from Slavery

Britain profited in many ways from the trade in slaves and the work that the slaves did in the colonies:

The Government – In 1770, the income from Jamaica alone was £1,500,000. In 1800 about 5% of the national income came from the trade in slaves and the West Indian colonies. Taxes and duties went to the government.

The Cities – Bristol and then Liverpool and London were the main cities involved. Liverpool entered the slave trade in the 1730s. By 1757 there were 176 Liverpool based slavers bringing a yearly profit of about a quarter of a million pounds. In 1785, Customs receipts on imported goods were £648,000.

Private Individuals – Planters from the colonies made huge fortunes and returned to live in Britain. They usually bought vast country estates and often built large houses in London, bought seats in Parliament, and lived in great luxury. William Beckford, a planter from Jamaica, was twice lord mayor of London. In 1769 he spent £10,000 (about $850,000 in today's prices) on one banquet. Three Beckfords were Members of Parliament in the 1750s.

A SOURCE

'Europe supported by Africa and America', an engraving by William Blake, 1796.

C SOURCE

There is hardly a ship comes to us (here in the Caribbean) but is half full at least with English commodities. Several score of thousands are employed in England in furnishing the plantations with all sorts of Necessaries, and these must be supplied with food. Moreover we take each year thousands of barrels of Irish beef, the price of which enables those people to pay their rents to their landlords that live and spend in England.

From 'The Groans of the Plantations' an anonymous 18th century pamphlet published in England.

B SOURCE

Warehouses built by Liverpool merchants, and named Gorée after a notorious slave trading center in West Africa.

Employment – In the slaving ports many people were employed in the trade. For example shipwrights, sailmakers, rope makers, provision merchants, dockers and sailors were all needed. Nearby towns also profited. Iron forgers, gunsmiths, weavers, potters and glassmakers all found new demands for their products. Manchester grew into a large city of mills making cloth from slave-grown cotton.

Investment – Planters and traders invested in manufacturing industries, banking and transport. The Phoenix Insurance Company and Barclays Bank were founded with sugar and slavery profits. John Gladstone, father of the future Prime Minister, invested profits from slave-worked plantations in a worldwide shipping and trading empire, including the Liverpool to Manchester Railway. Docks, warehouses, canals and railways were all built with money coming from slavery.

E The fruit of the labor of these slaves has long been the means of making us slaves at home.

William Cobbett, speaking about working conditions in Britain, around 1820.

The Barclay Brothers

The Barclay brothers belonged to the Society of Friends, or Quaker, religion. In the 1750s, they traded in slaves and other goods in the USA and the Caribbean. David Barclay owned a plantation in Jamaica. After the Quakers renounced slavery he freed all his slaves. The family's wealth was put into the manufacture of textiles and iron, which were widely used in the slave trade. They also started Barclays Bank.

Fonthill Abbey in Wiltshire, built by the Beckford family in the 1790s. It eventually fell down because of bad foundations.

D

3.5 The War of American Independence

A map of the United States of America before the Civil War, showing the original 13 colonies, slave owning and free states.

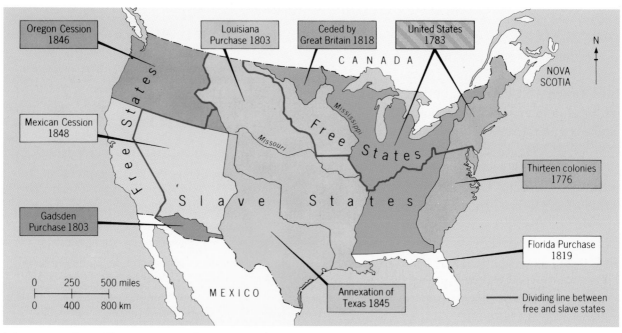

Many people in Europe wanted to escape from constant wars and religious persecution. They, and others who wanted a better life, went to North America. The first settlers were soon joined by many others. They wanted more and more land to make money. They were resisted by Native Americans, who believed that the land belonged to the Great Spirit. People should only use it to feed themselves.

The British fought Native Americans and the French for control. They promised slaves freedom if they fought, killed or captured an enemy. To pay for these wars, the British government increased the taxes the colonists paid. The colonists were unhappy about this, since the customs service was strengthened and they were obliged to provide free quarters and supplies for British troops. Soon there was a full-scale war between the colonists and the British Government, the **War of American Independence**.

Lord Dunmore, the Governor of Virginia, announced that he would free any slave who fought for Britain. The settlers' leader, **George Washington**, reluctantly decided to allow slaves into his army. The British lost the war and left. Some of the settlers' slaves/soldiers were freed, some were not. Some of the free Blacks came to Britain, others went to Canada.

A

SOURCE

This slave's back was scarred by years of whipping. This picture was originally in 'Harpers Weekly', 1863.

On 4 July 1776, the colonists' **Declaration of Independence** said 'that all men are created equal...with certain unalienable Rights, that among these are Life, Liberty and the Pursuit of Hapiness'. However slaves were not counted as men. Hungry for land, the European immigrants spread further and further west. Those who owned slaves took them. Some free Blacks also moved west.

Some states abolished slavery. Some new states were 'free' which meant that slavery was prohibited, but some had laws stopping Blacks from entering. Congress was dominated by the Southern States which depended on slave labor for their wealth. In 1793 the **Fugitive Slave Law** was passed; this made it illegal to shelter runaway slaves or prevent their capture. In 1820 Congress voted to keep new states 'free' north of the Missouri river, but in 1854 this law was rejected. North-South tensions were increased by the 1857 Dred Scott decision, which said that slavery could not be banned in the territories, and that the US Constitution had not forseen Blacks being given citizenship.

An unknown Black person protesting about slavery, quoted in a book published in 1810.

B

SOURCE

A Black seaman from the American War of Independence.

Banneker

Benjamin Banneker (1731–1806) is probably the best known Black person in early US history. He was an astronomer, surveyor, mathematician and farmer. In 1753 he built a clock made entirely of wood, which kept perfect time for 50 years. He used only a pocket watch and a picture of a clock as models. Based on his own observations, he created an almanac of tidal and astronomical calculations and weather predictions. He sent it to Thomas Jefferson, at the same time calling for the abolition of slavery and for liberal attitudes towards Blacks.

On Jefferson's recommendation, in 1791 President Washington appointed him to help survey the layout of the new capital city, Washington DC. Banneker's work was used by abolitionists as evidence of Blacks' talents.

3.6 Resistance in North America

Slaves in North America resisted slavery in as many ways as slaves in the Caribbean did. Two of the largest revolts were in the early 19th century. In 1800 Gabriel Prosser organized at least a thousand slaves in Richmond, Virginia, to attack the city. The plan was betrayed. The Governor called out troops. The slaves were defeated. Thirty five, including Prosser, were executed. In 1822 in Charleston, South Carolina, Denmark Vesey plotted a rising of slaves. He had bought his freedom and gained some education. He sought help from Haiti and took four years to perfect his plan. The plan involved so many, however, that it was difficult to keep it secret. The Whites heard about it, rounded up suspects and executed 47.

A **SOURCE**

We have closed every avenue by which light (knowledge and understanding) might enter the slaves' minds. If you could extinguish the capacity to see the light we should be safe.

A Virginia politician in the 1830s.

B **SOURCE**

If he makes an effort (to escape) and fails he will be beaten unmercifully by the master. If he does get away what will he find? He is ignorant of the world. All the White part of mankind that he has ever seen are enemies. The master tells him that abolitionists decoy slaves into the free states to catch them and sell them to Louisiana or Mississippi. If he goes to Canada, the British will put him in a mine underground for life with both eyes put out.

Lewis Clarke talking about his fears, before escaping from slavery (in the 1840s).

C **SOURCE**

The Seminole War in 1836.

Harriet Tubman – an outstanding woman who helped many slaves escape. She is shown with some of the slaves she helped to free.

Escaping slaves were often helped by Native Americans. Many went to Spanish-held Florida and joined the **Seminole** nation. In 1819 the United States bought Florida. Because the US wanted to expand its territory and because the people who lived in Georgia were afraid to be so close to free Blacks, US troops tried for 20 years to conquer them. In 1841 the Seminoles accepted an offer of peace and moved, with the Black members of the nation, to 'Indian Territory' in Oklahoma and Arkansas.

It is estimated that in the 19th century between 40,000 and 100,000 slaves escaped to the free states in the North and to Canada. Many were helped by the network of people and places known as the **Underground Railroad**. These people included some slaves as well as free Blacks and some Whites. They hid, clothed, fed, advised and guided the runaways to the next safe haven on the long and dangerous journey to safety.

One of the most famous 'conductors' was **Harriet Tubman**. She was born a slave in about 1820 in Maryland. She resisted slavery in every way she could. Her owner said she was 'stupid' and 'not worth sixpence'. In 1849, when her owner died, Harriet ran away. The Underground Railroad helped her to reach Canada. She could not forget her family and friends back in Maryland and so became a conductor, making 19 journeys to Maryland. She led 300 people to safety. Southerners offered rewards of $52,000 for her capture but she always eluded them and never lost a 'passenger'.

Turner

Nat Turner (1800–31) led the most dangerous rebellion in US history. The rebellion took place in 1831 in Southampton County, Virginia. Turner was a religious, intelligent man, determined to fight slavery. Turner believed that God had chosen him to destroy the plantation owners. He later said that he was told to 'arise and slay his enemies with their own weapons'.

With a small group of followers, Turner first killed his master and his master's family. The rebels eventually murdered about 60 Whites, the largest number in any slave rebellion. The Virginia militia hunted Turner down. He and over 20 other rebels were hanged. Angry Whites killed nearly 100 innocent slaves. As a result of the rebellion, Southern states passed strict laws to limit the freedoms of Blacks, especially those of preachers.

3.7 Free People of African Descent

North America to 1860

Freedom did not mean **equality** either in the North or the South of the USA. There was **segregation** (separation) of Blacks and Whites. Blacks had separate schools, churches and even burial grounds. Segregation was the law in the South and custom in the North. In most states free Blacks could not vote, sit on juries or stand for election. Throughout the 19th century new European immigrants to the USA, many of whom were poor, feared competition from Blacks. They voted to limit Blacks' rights and to stop them working in some trades and professions. From the 1830s there were anti-Black riots in the North.

To deal with this situation, Black people set up their own institutions, including schools. Southern Whites hit back by passing laws that did not allow more than five Blacks to study together, and in 1831 some states banned the education of Blacks altogether. Black churches, mainly Methodist and Baptist, were set up in many places. Colleges were started to train ministers and missionaries to send to Africa. From the 1780s Blacks formed social and political societies which, with the churches, often set up schools and self-help societies. Many became involved in the **abolition** movement, which campaigned to stop the slave trade.

A **SOURCE**

Even the noblest Black is denied that which is free to the vilest White. The omnibus, the ballot-box, the jury box, the army, the school, the church, the social circle and the table are all either absolutely or virtually denied him.

Gerritt Smith, a New York abolitionist, in 1835.

B **SOURCE**

A respectable master mechanic told us that in 1830 the President of a Mechanical Association was publicly tried by the Society for the crime of assisting a Colored young man to learn a trade. Such was the feeling among the mechanics that no Colored boy could learn a trade, or Colored journeyman find employment.

A Report in 1834 which investigated the conditions under which free Blacks lived in Cincinnati, Ohio.

C **SOURCE**

New York mobs lynch a Black man in 1863. Anti-Black riots rocked many Northern cities before, during and after the Civil War.

Some groups sponsored **colonization**. These organizations wanted to take Blacks back to Africa. Generally they were more popular with Whites than with most Blacks. Some societies did set up African-American settlements in Liberia in West Africa. In 1815, Paul Cuffee, a wealthy Black land and shipowner, settled 38 immigrants in Sierra Leone at his own expense. He set up a business exporting African goods to the United States, the West Indies and Europe.

Businessmen like Cuffee were rare; banks would not lend money to Blacks to start businesses. Another successful man was James Forten, who had served in the US Navy. He invented and manufactured a device that helped control the sails on ships. By the 1830s he had built up a large fortune, most of which he gave to the abolition movement.

Martin Delany was one of the few Black professional men. He studied medicine and law at Harvard University and became an internationally known writer and **abolitionist**. During the American Civil War he was made the first Black army officer. After the war he was appointed as a judge.

Abraham Camp of Illinois, writing to the Secretary of the Colonization Society in 1818.

E

SOURCE

Martin Delany, wearing the uniform of a US Army officer.

F

SOURCE

Year	Total	% Free
USA		
1790	757,000	8
1830	2,329,000	14
1860	4,442,000	11
The South		
1790	690,000	5
1830	2,162,000	8
1860	4,097,000	6
The North		
1790	67,000	40
1830	167,000	83
1860	345,000	67

The Black population of the United States

Delany

Martin Delany (1812–85) was born in Charleston, West Virginia. He became famous as a Black social reformer, doctor, journalist and army officer. He practiced medicine in Pittsburgh but spent most of his time fighting against slavery. He worked for the Underground Railroad and wrote for the abolitionist newspaper owned by Frederick Douglass.

In the 1850s Delany joined a movement that urged all free Blacks to return to Africa, but later lost his enthusiasm for this movement. He joined the Union Army during the American Civil War and served as a surgeon. He was the first Black to be promoted to the rank of Major. This was a significant achievement at a time when Blacks were still generally seen as menial labourers, looked down upon and badly treated. Delany stands out as one of the first Blacks in the USA to join the professional classes and to become a respected figure in society.

4.1 Opposition to Slavery in Britain

Not everyone agreed with the trade in human beings. In 1776 **Adam Smith** wrote that slave-worked economies were, in the end, not economical, because an unpaid worker doesn't work hard. The **Quaker** and **Methodist** churches spoke out against slavery. In the 1770s, **Granville Sharp** began a campaign against slavery in the courts of law. Others joined in, including two African ex-slaves, **Ottobah Cugoano** and **Olaudah Equiano**.

In 1787 the **Abolition Society** was formed. Its secretary, **Thomas Clarkson**, traveled through Britain converting people to the cause and persuading them not to use slave-grown sugar. **William Wilberforce** was their main spokesperson in Parliament. In 1807 the campaign was successful and the slave trade was abolished. The British Government then tried to persuade other countries to do the same. Most, including the USA, agreed. Many traders, however, defied the law and continued to export humans to the Americas.

Abolition of the slave trade did not mean freedom for slaves. Other campaigners, including women like **Elizabeth Coltman**, took up the cause of **emancipation** (the freeing of all slaves).

A

SOURCE

The claim to own a Negro, like a horse or a dog, is defective. It cannot be justified unless you can prove that a Negro slave is neither man, woman nor child. The poor Negro has not been guilty of any offenses for which he might lawfully lose his humanity. Therefore it must be recognised that he differs from a horse or a dog in this essential point – he is a **human being**.

From a pamphlet by Granville Sharp, a British anti-slavery campaigner, published in 1769.

B *'A slave in chains'. From an anti-slavery book of 1827. William Cowper was a popular poet.*

SOURCE

I WOULD NOT HAVE A SLAVE TO TILL MY GROUND
TO CARRY ME, TO FAN ME WHILE I SLEEP,
AND TREMBLE WHEN I WAKE, FOR ALL
    THE WEALTH
THAT SINEWS BOUGHT AND SOLD,
    HAVE EVER EARN'D.
WE HAVE NO SLAVES AT HOME –
    WHY THEN ABROAD?

COWPER.

C **SOURCE**

To the captains employed in the slave trade, every merchant who is engaged in the slave trade and every gentleman that has an estate in our plantations – Is there a God? Is He a just God? Then there must be a state of retribution. Then what reward will He render you? Think now, 'He shall have judgement without mercy that showed no mercy.'

John Wesley, the founder of Methodism, arguing against slavery in 1774.

D **SOURCE**

Men propose only **gradually** to abolish the worst of crimes. I trust no Ladies Association for the Emancipation of Slavery will ever be found with such words attached to it.

An anonymous pamphlet, published in London in 1826.

E **SOURCE**

Continuing the cultivation of the West Indian Islands will be impossible without importing slaves. Without slaves the crops would decline and the population become extinct. Discontent and dissatisfaction may dismember the empire and the people renounce their counry and take refuge in a neighboring kingdom.

William Beckford, a poor relative of the millionaire planter of the same name, 1790.

Parliament was reformed in 1832. New MPs were elected from industrial areas. They wanted to stop Government restrictions on trade and bring in **free trade**. This meant that merchants could buy and sell anywhere, for the best prices. West Indian sugar would compete in a free market. Even freed slaves could be customers! The Caribbean colonies were becoming expensive to run. The plantations were inefficient and it cost too much to put down slave revolts. The anti-slavery movement gained strength, drawing inspiration from religious feeling and encouragement from other pressures for reform. Slavery had to go! Hundreds of thousands of people signed petitions against slavery.

The **Emancipation Act** to free the slaves was passed in 1833. According to the Act, slaves had to serve an 'apprenticeship' of seven years before they were completely free. While apprenticed, they had to work three quarters of their time (40 hours) for their ex-owners. The owners got £20 million in compensation; the slaves were given nothing.

Sharp

Granville Sharp (1735–1813) was a leading British abolitionist. He became a lawyer and was very active in the anti-slavery movement. Defending a Black immigrant in 1772, Sharp won an important legal decision that stated as soon as any slave set foot in England he became free.

Sharp's most famous case concerned the slave ship *Zong*. In 1781, 131 slaves were thrown overboard to save water supplies. The case ended without settlement but Sharp, who was told about the *Zong* by Olaudah Equiano, was able to heighten public awareness of the cruelty of the slave trade. The case for abolition was advanced.

4.2 Opposition to Slavery in the USA

The 1787 Constitution of the United States of America freed Whites from British domination, but did not free slaves. Freed Black war veterans and other Black leaders sent petitions to the US Congress and the governments of each state, asking for freedom. They published books, pamphlets and a newspaper called *Freedom's Journal*. In 1829, David Walker called for Blacks to rise up. He warned White Americans that not freeing slaves would end in disaster.

Anti-slavery Whites formed **abolitionist societies**. Most societies did not admit Blacks or women and promoted the 'colonization' (immigration) of Blacks to Liberia and elsewhere. In 1833 the American Anti-Slavery Society was founded with both Black and White membership. Their fight against slavery was far more whole-hearted. Abolitionists were viciously attacked in the South and the North (where they were feared as disturbers of the Union and traditions). Some went to Europe to ask for support.

Abolitionist Robert Pleasants in 1785.

Frederick Douglass, a powerful abolitionist agitator.

C SOURCE

B SOURCE

Sojourner Truth, a runaway slave who became a popular speaker at abolitionist rallies.

Reverend T. S. Wright attacking racial prejudice, 1837.

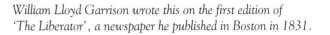

William Lloyd Garrison wrote this on the first edition of 'The Liberator', a newspaper he published in Boston in 1831.

One of the best known anti-slavery speakers was **Sojourner Truth**. She was born a slave in 1790. She escaped and joined the movements campaigning for freedom and for equal rights for women. Another powerful speaker against slavery and segregation was **Frederick Douglass.** Also born a slave, he ran away and, with the help of the Underground Railroad, reached free Massachusetts. He traveled to Britain many times and his speeches drew large, admiring audiences. In 1847, with Martin Delany, he started a newspaper, *The North Star.*

In 1850 the **Fugitive Slave Law** was made stronger to recapture runaways. Violence erupted in the streets as opponents fought off the slave catchers. There were also fights in the new territory of Kansas which continued for four years, over whether Kansas should enter the United States as a free or slave state. The newly formed **Republican Party** promised to stop the spread of slavery. Its leader, **Abraham Lincoln**, was elected President of the United States in 1860. The stage was set for a major clash between abolitionists and supporters of slavery.

F

SOURCE

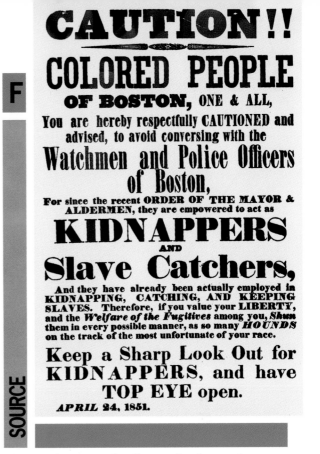

A poster that appeared in Boston after slave catchers came to the city and captured Thomas Sims, a Black runaway, and took him back to Georgia.

G

Sojourner Truth

Isabella Baumfree (about 1797–1883) was born a slave but was freed in 1828 when New York banned slavery. In 1843 she felt God had commanded her to preach. She took the name Sojourner Truth and traveled widely, speaking for the abolition of slavery and for women's rights. She attracted admiring audiences. She visited Washington in 1864, to help Blacks from the South find jobs and homes.

SOURCE

A contemporary print of Black escapers from Virginia defending themseves against slave catchers in Maryland, 1853. Wesley Harris, at the front, escaped.

4.3 Opposition to Slavery in the Caribbean

News of the success of the revolution in Haiti and of the abolition of the slave trade by the British government spread through the British colonies. The Whites feared the effect these events would have on their slaves.

In 1815 about 250 slaves plotted to kill all the whites in Jamaica. They were found out and the leader was sentenced to death, and his deputy was transported to Australia. The slaves were not put off by this; in 1823 and 1824 there were more conspiracies – with similar results.

There were also plots in other colonies – Barbados in 1816, British Guiana in 1823 and Antigua in 1831. In Trinidad there was constant fighting between troops and runaway slaves between 1819 and 1829.

In the 1820s and 1830s the British government ordered that slave conditions should be improved in the colonies it ruled directly. It also asked self-governing colonies to pass similar laws. People in Britain campaigned for **emancipation**. The White planters grew more and more fearful. Slaves and **freedmen** (freed Blacks) who had learned to read (taught mainly by missionaries), read, discussed and spread the news from Britain. The rumor spread that emancipation would happen soon. In Jamaica, Whites held meetings to protest about what the British government was doing and what its intentions might be.

A **SOURCE**

The undaunted bravery and fortitude with which many of the rebels met their fate was very remarkable. It strikingly showed the difficulties that follow the continuation of slavery now that the spirit of freedom has spread. Many of the Negroes had learned to prefer death to bondage.

From 'Death Struggles of Slavery' by the Reverend Henry Bleby, 1853. He witnessed the executions of the Montego Bay rebels.

B **SOURCE**

I would rather die upon yon gallows than live in slavery.

Sam Sharpe, while awaiting execution, 1832.

Rebels destroying a road (right) and a wharf (flames, center) during the 1831 rebellion in Jamaica.

C **SOURCE**

D

Head-Quarters, Montego-Bay,
St. James's, Jan. 2, 1832.

TO

THE REBELLIOUS SLAVES.

NEGROES,

YOU have taken up arms against your Masters, and have burnt and plundered their Houses and Buildings. Some wicked persons have told you that the King has made you free, and that your Masters withhold your freedom from you. In the name of the King, I come amongst you, to tell you that you are misled. I bring with me numerous Forces to punish the guilty, and all who are found with the Rebels will be put to death, without Mercy. You cannot resist the King's Troops. Surrender yourselves, and beg that your crime may be pardoned. All who yield themselves up at any Military Post *immediately*, provided they are not principals and chiefs in the burnings that have been committed, will receive His Majesty's gracious pardon. All who hold out, will meet with certain death.

WILLOUGHBY COTTON,
Maj. General Command.

GOD SAVE THE KING.

A proclamation to the rebel slaves.

E

The revolt failed but dealt a further wound to slavery. The evidence taken before Parliament made it clear that if the abolition of slavery were not speedily done by law, the slaves would take matters into their own hands and bring their bondage to a violent and bloody end.

From 'Death Struggles of Slavery' by the Reverend Henry Bleby, 1853.

In Montego Bay, in 1831, hundreds of slaves joined together and agreed to refuse to work after Christmas. They were led by **Sam 'Daddy' Sharpe**, a slave who was a Baptist lay preacher and could both read and write. Sharpe appointed captains in all parts of western Jamaica to lead the rebels in case of attack by military forces. Some free Blacks also joined in.

About 20,000 slaves refused to work on December 27. The local militia was called out first and then the British troops stationed in Jamaica. It took the soldiers two months to defeat the rebels. They had caused over a million pounds worth of damage to planters' property and the military operations cost £162,000. Two hundred and seventy two rebels were executed, including one woman; 21 were transported to prison colonies. Dozens of slaves were imprisoned with hard labor or were punished with up to 300 lashes. Sam Sharpe was executed on May 23 1832.

The harshness of these punishments did not prevent further unrest in Jamaica and other islands. The British government got the message clearly. Within a year the **Emancipation Act** was passed to free the slaves.

Sharpe

Sam Sharpe (died 1832) was born a slave in Jamaica. He was a field hand and could read and write. He became a lay preacher and head deacon at the Reverend Thomas Burchell's Baptist church in Montego Bay. Sharpe was known for his voice. He amazed people by the power and freedom with which he spoke. He was able to have 'the feelings and passions of his hearers completely at his command'. His owners allowed him to visit other plantations at night to preach. Sharpe used this freedom to enlist other Baptists into his secret army to fight for freedom, and appointed captains to recruit and train others to take part in his great rebellion.

The 'Baptist War' shook Jamaica. There were 500 killings and executions. The Reverend Henry Bleby visited Sharpe in jail as he waited for his execution. Sharpe was described by him as 'the most intelligent and remarkable slave I ever met. He possessed intellectual and oratorical powers above the common order. He thought, and he learnt from the Bible, that the Whites had no more right to hold Black people in slavery, than the Black people had to make the White people slaves.' Sam Sharpe was hanged. The planters seemed addicted to the bloody habits of the past. Many people in Britain were outraged. One week after Sharpe died the British Parliament appointed a committee to consider ways of ending slavery.

5.1 Apprenticeship and After

Plantation owners in the Caribbean were furious about losing their free labor when the slaves were emancipated in 1833. They complained that the £20 million they got in compensation from the British government was not enough.

The 'apprentices' were also unhappy. The **Emancipation Act** was unclear on many points. How much work did they have to do in the 40 hours that they had to give to their masters? Could they do it all in four days so that there were more full days to earn money for themselves? Did their time include traveling to the fields if these were miles away? Did they have the right to bargain for better wages?

The British government appointed Special Magistrates to decide arguments. There were not enough of them and their power was limited. The Assemblies of planters which governed most of the colonies passed laws to make sure that there were always workers available. Anyone found without a job was called a vagrant and punished severely. Whipping and the treadmill were commonly used. High taxes were put on Black smallholders (people who had small farms). Small traders were made to pay for a license to do business. To avoid discontent from the 'apprentices' and the interference of the Special Magistrates, all the Assemblies ended apprenticeship by 1838. The Special Magistrates were sacked.

The Assemblies now felt that they could do what they liked. They increased taxes and the cost of trading licenses. Immigration was forbidden. Planters charged high rents for homes and land and paid very low wages. People who rented property could be thrown out at one week's notice. Planters refused to sell land in the small plots that the freedmen could afford to buy.

A SOURCE

Planting sugar cane in Antigua. Black people had to do back-breaking work like this both before and after emancipation. Print by W. Clark, 1823.

B SOURCE

What a difficult and critical task is mine! First to maintain the rights of the Negroes, without irritating the planters. Next to calm the planters' tempers and combat their prejudices, while at the same time upholding their legal claims to their apprentices. Above all, to bring about a kind feeling between parties at present hating each other.

Major Colthurst, a Special Magistrate in Barbados and St Vincent, February, 1836.

To escape from this hopeless situation, people **squatted** on any free or unused land that they could find. This land was often poor quality and a long way from the markets. Squatting led to trouble with the police. Squatters also couldn't vote. To vote it was necessary to own land and pay taxes.

Protestant missionaries were the only source of help. **Methodists**, **Baptists** and **Moravians** bought large areas of land which they divided up into small plots that people could buy. The missionaries also loaned the money to help people set up as small farmers. Missionaries started schools. They advised the freedmen how to deal with employers and injustice. The planters hated the missionaries and feared the Blacks. This tense and uneasy situation was likely to explode.

C   **SOURCE**

Daily wages	
Antigua	9d (6¢)
Nevis	6d (4¢)
Trinidad	2s 1d (17¢)
Jamaica	1s 6d (12¢)

Prices	
Yam	2d (1¢) per lb
Flour	4d (3¢) per lb
Beef	9d (6¢) per lb
Boots	5s 3d (43¢) pair
Rent	1s 6d (12¢) week

Wages and prices in the British West Indies around 1842.

D   **SOURCE**

All the agitation is well known to the apprentices. If full freedom is not conceded next August, I would give little for West Indian property. The planters look grave. It is all their own fault.

Major Colthurst on Barbados, April 1838.

E   **SOURCE**

A voter must own property worth £6 a year or pay £20 rent. There are probably 50,000 people in Jamaica who qualify but there are only 3,000 voters. A tax of ten shillings (50p) per person to register explains the difference.

W. G. Sewell, an American journalist traveling in the West Indies, 1858–60.

F   **SOURCE**

The memorial plaque to the son of William Knibb, a Baptist Missionary, in Falmouth, Jamaica.

Hill

Richard Hill was born in Jamaica in 1795. His father was a wealthy Englishman and his mother was part African, part Indian. Hill was sent to England to be educated. His father told him that he should struggle for the freedom of his race. Hill went to Cuba and North America to study slaves' conditions. In Britain he became a leader of the anti-slavery struggle. He gave Parliament a petition for no restrictions on free Colored people and for the freeing of slaves. He went to Haiti to study further. Back in London he fought until emancipation in 1834, then helped settle disputes between ex-slaves and ex-masters in Jamaica.

5.2 The Morant Bay Rebellion

George William Gordon was the illegitimate son of a wealthy planter and a slave woman. He worked hard and became a dealer in land and property, and a produce merchant. His business did well. He bought his mother's and sisters' freedom and had his sisters educated in England. Then he bought a plantation. He was appointed one of the magistrates for St Thomas-in-the-East, his home district in Jamaica. He also became a Baptist and a leader of the **radical** wing of one of the two Jamaican political parties, the Town Party. The Party's members were mainly mixed-race townsmen such as merchants, officials and lawyers.

Gordon and his fellow radicals became spokesmen for the poor people who had no vote. In 1862 Governor Eyre removed Gordon from his post as a magistrate. The next year Gordon won a seat in Jamaica's Assembly for the district of **Morant Bay**. In the Assembly, Gordon spoke against Governor Eyre and his policies.

In the 1860s, conditions in Jamaica were very bad. Drought affected plantation owners and small farmers alike. But the small farmers also faced injustice. They paid heavier taxes than the planters. They farmed the poorest soil, as neither planters nor the government would sell fertile land to the Black population. There were many protests; a petition was sent to Queen Victoria in Britain.

He had dreamt of regenerating the Negro race by baptising them in English Radicalism. He would have brought nothing but confusion and precipitated Jamaica into anarchy. But to hang him was an extreme measure.

James A. Froude, Professor of History at Oxford University, writing about Gordon in 1888.

Paul Bogle.

Paul Bogle was a farmer, a Baptist lay preacher and Gordon's campaign manager. In 1865 he led a delegation to see Governor Eyre. The Governor refused to see them so Gordon began collecting money to send a delegation to England. The Governor heard rumors that Bogle was gathering arms to drive the Europeans from the island. The **Custos** (Chief Magistrate of a district) sent eight policemen to arrest Bogle.

Bogle and his friends were ready for them. They captured three policemen and sent them back to the Custos with a message that they would come the next day to Morant Bay to discuss recent injustices. Bogle and 300 other armed men approached the town square. They were warned not to enter but disobeyed and the militia opened fire. In the fighting, the Custos and 26 other people were killed. Governor Eyre declared **martial law**. He sent troops and a naval vessel to Morant Bay. The militia and the soldiers went on the rampage, killing people and burning houses as they searched for Bogle and other 'rebels'.

The Governor arrested Gordon, who had been in Kingston, the capital, during the fighting. Although there was no evidence that Gordon had any involvement, he was court-martialed in Morant Bay for stirring up rebellion and hanged on October 23, 1865. Bogle was also hanged. Six hundred Blacks were flogged, 580 killed or hanged. Over 1,000 homes were burned.

Lieutenant Adcock's report on operations against Bogle and his followers. Adcock was a Lieutenant in the British Army.

Eyre

Edward J. Eyre had been a British official in Australia, New Zealand and the West Indies. He was intolerant and weak. In 1862 Eyre became Governor of Jamaica, which had problems like drought and high prices. Eyre antagonized the Assembly and removed its leader, George William Gordon, from his post as magistrate. One thing led to another – riots, court cases, stone throwing, calling out the militia and shooting – and the Jamaica Rebellion of 1865 began.

Eyre frantically called for military reinforcements. Gordon was arrested and hanged. Hundreds of Blacks died. A Royal Commission found that the punishments were excessive, but Eyre escaped the charge of murdering Gordon. Eyre was dismissed as a result of the rebellion but then lived on a comfortable pension.

D **SOURCE**

Paul Bogle's hanging in front of the Court House at Morant Bay, which was burnt out in the fight between Bogle and the militia.

5.3 The Results of the Rebellion

The Morant Bay 'Rebellion' and its cruel suppression had widespread results. Governor Eyre was recalled to Britain. Fearing further outbreaks of trouble, many Assemblies told the British government they wanted to go back to being a Crown Colony. This meant that a British-appointed governor ruled, advised by a Council which he chose. It was not until the end of the 19th century that very limited democracy was restored.

The British government realized that conditions had to be improved. Medical services and a unified police force were set up. The government, not the planters, appointed judges to the new district courts. Government savings banks were set up to help the poorer people. An Agricultural Research Institute was opened. New Public Works Departments built roads and maintained public buildings. However, the islands' income was often so low that many of the reforms were abandoned.

One of the British government's main concerns was to prevent further outbreaks of lawlessness. Blacks had to be made to accept their poverty and an inferior status. It was decided that this could best be done through education. New schools were built. Mission schools were given money if they agreed to follow the new education policy.

Children were taught basic reading, writing and arithmetic. They were trained in 'industrious working habits' and taught 'prompt and cheerful obedience' to their superiors. They were told that all Whites were superior. Everything British was superior. They learned that the new languages developing in the Caribbean were inferior. The new religions, a mixture of African and Christian, were inferior and wicked. Children were taught that anything coming from Europe was much better than anything or anyone of African descent.

A SOURCE

Let the colored men of Jamaica be true to themselves, and their progress will be certain. Their best policy is to form a bond of union with their White brethren. If this is done, no Governor will keep from them the rights to which they are entitled as loyal subjects.

John Costello, a mixed-race member of the Jamaican Assembly, 1862.

B SOURCE

If the British Government take over the island, they will be guided by the landowners. The British Parliament will never allow the island to be placed in the hands of those who have no property.

H. A. Whitelocke, the planters' leader, speaking in the Jamaica Assembly, 1865.

C SOURCE

Kingston, Jamaica in 1860.

Only about half the children who had been enrolled actually attended school. Many parents could not afford the fees. Eventually the British government stopped fees in an effort to get children into school. As one magistrate said, a 'carefully nurtured sense of inferiority' had to be taught to the Black children.

Strikes and riots went on; poverty and homelessness grew. Early in the 20th century the British government decided that the attempt to keep Blacks down by using education had not been very successful. Spending on 'law and order' went up and spending on education went down. The Councils did not mind as they were afraid for their property and their wealth.

D

SOURCE

A country school in Jamaica about 1900.

Thomas

John Jacob Thomas (1840–89) was born in Trinidad. He went to the new 'teachers' training college' there. He had his first teaching job in 1860. Thomas then moved to the civil service. His fame came from writing his book, *Theory and Practice of Creole Grammar*. He went to England to lecture on his work. He then returned to Trinidad where illness forced him to retire, but he continued to speak and write about education. J. J. Froude, from Oxford University, wrote a book that insulted West Indians. Thomas wrote a reply, 'Froudacity', contradicting the insult. He returned to England to work on a book about the study of language, but died there of tuberculosis in 1889.

5.4 Labor and Economy

Drought and hurricanes hit the Caribbean in the 1860s and affected both planters and Black small farmers. Even more damaging were the effects of the free trade policy followed by Britain and a world-wide drop in sugar prices. The worst affected island was Jamaica, which had the highest production costs (i.e. it was expensive to cultivate and harvest the sugar crop). Jamaica could not compete with Cuba, which used more modern technology as well as slaves to produce sugar. Jamaica also faced competition from European sugar beet and cane from India. Hundreds of planters left Jamaica and the other islands; others tried to change to crops like coffee, cocoa and cotton.

Trinidad and British Guiana were in a different position. They had only recently started growing sugar. How could they get a supply of cheap labor? The slave trade was abolished. The other colonies prevented Blacks immigrating in order to keep wages low. At first the new colonies imported Africans who had been freed from slave ships by the Royal Navy. But there were not enough, so they turned to India. About half a million Indians were imported as indentured laborers. The scheme was stopped in 1917 when the Indian government complained to the British government about the appalling living and working conditions of the Indian workers in the colonies.

B SOURCE

1840	49s 1d	($4.17)
1841	39s 8d	($3.31)
1842	36s 11d	($3.14)
1843	33s 9d	($2.79)
1844	33s 8d	($2.86)
1845	32s 11d	($2.81)
1846	34s 5d	($2.92)
1847	28s 3d	($2.40)
1848	23s 8d	($2.00)

Average price, per 50 kilos (approximately), of cane sugar in Britain in the 1840s.

C SOURCE

Jamaica	22s 7d	($1.92)
Trinidad	25s 0d	($2.13)
Barbados	15s 5d	($1.31)
Grenada	16s 2d	($1.38)
Tobago	17s 0d	($1.45)
Cuba	12s 0d	($1.02)

Approximate cost of producing 50 kilos of sugar in 1848.

A SOURCE

Indian laborers breaking cocoa pods in Trinidad.

D SOURCE

	1852	1890
Sugar from colonies	85	15
Sugar from foreign producers	13	21
Beet sugar from Europe	2	64
	100%	100%

Kinds of sugar used in Britain (shown as a percentage).

E **SOURCE**

The average Jamaican peasants, owning one or two acres, grow provisions for themselves and families, and for the village market. They raise for sale coffee, pimento, arrow-root, fruit, vegetables and sometimes sugar cane. They have their horses and their stock.

William G. Sewell describing life in Jamaica on his journey through the West Indies 1858–60.

The small farmers sold what they did not eat at local markets. Some grew sugar cane, coffee or ginger for export. In 1870 an American sea captain named Baker discovered that he could sell Jamaican bananas in Boston for a tremendous profit. Farmers quickly switched to growing bananas. Captain Baker made so much money that he was able to buy up abandoned plantations with good soil. The small farmers couldn't grow bananas as cheaply. This was the beginning of large scale fruit farming in the Caribbean by American companies.

Black West Indians without land had to take any job at any wage. The British government did not allow manufacturing in the colonies so most jobs were very low paid seasonal agricultural work. From 1895 workers organized strikes and formed trade unions. British trades unions would not help them so they sought help from the American Federation of Labor. The White rulers saw this as more disloyal than the actual strikes. The employers broke every strike by sacking all the workers and getting others to do the work.

Times were hard for the Blacks, except for a very few who managed to earn a reasonable living. The mixed-race population and even the few Blacks who had been educated into the professions in Britain found things just as difficult. There was a surplus population with no prospects. Eventually the anti-immigration laws were removed.

F **SOURCE**

When White planters refuse to associate with Colored planters, White merchants with Colored merchants, and White mechanics with Colored mechanics, simply because they are Colored, the question ceases to be a social one, and assumes a dangerous political complexion.

From 'The Ordeal of Free Labor in the West Indies' by William G. Sewell, 1862. Sewell was an American journalist who wrote for 'The New York Times'.

Mills

Walter Mills led the first Working Man's Association in the West Indies, which was formed in 1897. He gave evidence to the Royal Commission to the British West Indies, which was investigating the effects of the depression in the sugar markets on the islands. His evidence was about poor sanitary conditions in houses both on sugar estates and in towns.

The Association also opposed the state-financed importation of laborers from India. This caused a surplus of labor, which brought about low wages. He asked that the government should establish a savings bank and that they should offer five acre plots and free plants to those laborers wishing to farm. The last idea was accepted by the British Royal Commission and put into action.

G **SOURCE**

Living conditions on the plantations around 1890 were often as bad as they had been during the days of slavery.

6.1 The United States – War and the North

The slave-owning Southern States, called the Confederacy, were worried that they would lose their power, perhaps even their slaves, under President Abraham Lincoln. They **seceded** (broke away) from the United States between November 1860 and February 1861. Civil war broke out in April.

The commanders of the Union (Northern States) Army disobeyed President Lincoln's order to return runaway slaves to the Confederacy. They called them 'contraband', set them free and let them join the Army. This and the need for more soldiers forced Lincoln to issue the **Emancipation Proclamation** in 1863, which freed all slaves in areas controled by the Confederacy. Blacks rushed to join up. A total of 178,985 fought in the war, one tenth of the Union Army. Thirty-seven thousand were killed in action and 17 Black soldiers and sailors were awarded the Congressional Medal of Honor, the highest award for bravery in the United States.

Black soldiers were in segregated regiments with White officers. There were protests, but by the end of the war in 1865, regiments were still segregated and only about 100 Black officers had been appointed. One of these was Major Martin Delany, the famous Black activist. Blacks protested about getting half the pay of White troops and having more 'fatigue' duties. Eventually Congress and the War Department had to agree to make Black and White soldiers' pay and work equal.

Black women also served in the Union forces. Harriet Tubman became a scout and led raids deep into Southern territory. Susie King Taylor, who escaped from Georgia, became a nurse, laundress and teacher to the 54th Massachusetts and the South Carolina regiments in which her uncles and brothers were soldiers.

A SOURCE

A Black corporal in the Union Army.

B SOURCE

At Helena they bore the brunt of the fighting and defeated a superior force of the enemy. Wherever the Negroes have had the chance they have shown the most exalted gallantry.

Newspaper comment on Black soldiers.

C

SOURCE

The 54th Massachusetts, a Black regiment, storming Fort Wagner in 1863. The print was made in 1889, based on a painting by an unknown journeyman artist. One of the regiment's soldiers won the Congressional Medal of Honor in the action.

The Confederate States refused to enlist Blacks into the Army but forced thousands to help the war effort as laborers. By March 1865 the South was losing the war so the Confederate President finally agreed that slaves should be recruited as soldiers. It was too late; in April the South gave in. Five days after the war ended, President Lincoln was assassinated.

In the North, anti-Black violence had grown. White workers feared that freed Blacks would cause wages to fall. There were serious riots in Detroit, Philadelphia, New York City, Buffalo and Brooklyn. Segregation stayed in place. Blacks demanded an end to discrimination and segregation.

Tubman

Araminta Tubman (1820–1913) was born in Maryland and worked as a weaver and housemaid. Her name was changed to Harriet, after her mother. At the age of eleven, when she was considered an adult slave, she worked in the fields. She escaped and became a conductor on the Underground Railroad. She worked as a nurse and a spy during the Civil War. After the War, the US Government would not give her the same benefits as men, so she joined the women's rights movement.

D

SOURCE

There are many people who do not know what some Southern Colored women did. Hundreds of them assisted Union soldiers by hiding them and helping them to escape.

From 'A Black Woman's Civil War Memoirs' by Susie King Taylor, 1902.

E

SOURCE

Men were killed and thrown in rivers, hung to trees and lamp posts, numbers shot down. No Black person could show but they were hunted down like wolves. This continued for four days.

Newspaper report of riots in New York in 1863.

A

SOURCE

Freedmen first voted in 1867–8. Ex-slaves were eager to vote.

B

SOURCE

The night school has been frequently disturbed. One evening a mob called out the teacher, confronted him with four revolvers and menacing expressions, demanding he quit the place and close the school. The freedmen promptly came to his aid.

A description of events in Florida in 1866 by Captain C. M. Hamilton.

Nine out of ten Black people in the USA lived in the rural South. The new President, Andrew Johnson, was a Southerner. He ordered that land given to freed Blacks be returned to the White planters. The defeated states were allowed to recall their state governments. These quickly passed laws forbidding Blacks to have **civil rights** like voting and education.

There was a struggle between the President and Congress over the post-war period, called **Reconstruction**. In 1866 Congress passed the **14th Amendment** to the US Constitution (1868) which granted equal civil rights and citizenship to Blacks. The **15th Amendment** (1870) gave equal voting rights to all men. Congress also opened up state lands in the South to Black settlers and set up the **Freedman's Bureau** to open hospitals and schools for Blacks, and to help them get employment and civil rights. Food was given to the poorest Blacks and Whites. The Freedmen's Bank (run by Whites) was opened, but it was badly managed and Black customers lost over $3 million.

Civil rights – rights belonging to any citizen, such as the right to vote, to a fair trial, to education, etc.

Reconstruction – the process of building up the whole United States again after the War. The Southern States had been badly damaged; Congress had to decide how to help them.

Amendment – a change or alteration to the Constitution of the United States, passed by Congress and three-quarters of the states.

Lynching – killing a person by 'mob justice', often for an imaginary crime and without a trial. Many blacks were lynched simply because of racial hatred.

Discrimination – unfair treatment of Blacks because of racial prejudice, e.g., Whites got the best jobs.

Reconciliation – peaceful settlement. The North chose to treat the South kindly and compromise over issues such as the treatment of Blacks, rather than forcing the Southern States to change.

The new opportunities were quickly seized. Black candidates were elected to Congress, state governments and city councils. Blacks set up farms and businesses, went to school and universities. This alarmed Southern Whites. Many joined anti-Black terrorist organizations like the Ku Klux Klan which attacked Blacks and pro-Black Whites. There were murders, lynchings, rapes and fires. There was increased **discrimination** as Whites gave Blacks only the worst jobs. Although Blacks were entitled to vote, armed gangs of Whites sometimes stopped them.

The US government in the North developed a spirit of **reconciliation** to the South, especially as there were opportunities to make money there. Congress closed the Freedman's Bureau and in 1875 the 15th Amendment was undermined when Congress rejected a Bill protecting Black voting rights. Laws were passed in the Southern States to enforce segregation. Marriage between Blacks and Whites was banned in some states. Southern states took away the Blacks' right to vote by imposing property and tax rules – and by violence. No Blacks were elected to Congress between 1901 and 1929. By 1910 it was impossible for most Blacks to vote. Many lost their property and returned to poverty.

D SOURCE

Members of the Ku Klux Klan. This organization carried out a campaign of terror and intimidation against Blacks and pro-Black Whites.

E

Well they were spitting in my face and throwing dirt in my eyes. When they had made me blind they busted open my cupboard and they eat all my pies up and took two pieces of meat. After a while they dragged me out into the big road, and they raped me out there.

Harriet Simril giving evidence to a Congressional committee that was investigating the Ku Klux Klan, 1871.

Forten

Charlotte Forten (1837–1914) was the granddaughter of James Forten, the Black businessman who gave much of his money to abolitionists. She was a teacher and taught free slaves during the Civil War. She wrote about her life and the needs of the South.

In Memphis, Tennessee, there was a reign of terror over the newly freed slaves.

C SOURCE

6.3 The United States to 1910

Segregation, loss of civil rights, violence and lynchings! How did Black people survive?

Some Blacks turned to education as a means of escape, but the state schools were overcrowded and teachers had little training. In the South the school year was often only three to four months long. Only about half the children were ever enrolled. State governments spent much less on the education of a Black child than a White one.

To overcome this problem, Black churches and organizations continued setting up their own schools. A Black woman, **Mary McLeod Bethune**, started the first high school for girls in Florida in 1904. By 1906 she had 250 pupils; by 1927 she had developed the school into a college. Another college principal, **Booker T. Washington**, was able to raise ample funds from wealthy Whites by publicly accepting segregation and only vocational education for Blacks. Students in Black colleges had to pay fees and even help raise money for new buildings, for example by forming choirs and giving concerts all over the USA and Europe. Other Blacks moved to cities in search of a better life. In 1890, 20% of Black people lived in cities. By 1910 it was 27%.

A SOURCE

Schools like this were set up for Black children and adults during Reconstruction.

B SOURCE

How hard many of these mothers work! Two girls graduated recently from Atlanta University. Their mother had been washing for several years to keep them in school. She came up to see them graduate. She was one of the happiest mothers I ever saw.

Samuel Barrows reporting a conversation he had with a Black clergyman in Chattanooga, Tennessee in 1891.

C SOURCE

On October 3, 1904, I opened the doors of my school with five girls enrolled. We burned logs and used the charred splinters as pencils and mashed elderberries for ink. I begged strangers for a broom and a lamp. I haunted the city dump and trash piles, retrieving discarded linen and kitchenware, cracked dishes, broken chairs. Everything was scoured and mended. In less than two years I had 250 pupils. To raise funds I rang doorbells, wrote articles and rode interminable miles on my old bicycle.

Mary McLeod Bethune describes the early days of her school and college.

D

SOURCE

Nat Love, the Black cowboy who became known as Deadwood Dick.

E

SOURCE

It seems to me that the horse chosen for me was the most vicious of the lot. I roped, threw, tied, bridled, saddled and mounted my mustang in exactly nine minutes. The time of my nearest competitor was twelve minutes and thirty seconds. This gave me the record and the Championship of the West, which I held up to the time that I quit the business in 1890, and my record has never been beaten.

From 'The Life and Adventures of Nat Love, by Himself', 1907.

Thousands of Black people moved to the West. Some had enough money to buy land. Those without money worked as farmhands or cowboys. One of the best known was Tennessee-born **Nat Love**. He moved to Kansas in 1869. He asked for a job with a Texas 'outfit' going home after a cattle drive. The trail boss said that he had to prove himself and gave Nat the roughest horse to ride. Nat was able to stay in the saddle and so he got the job. In 1876 he won prizes for roping wild horses and in a shooting match. He was given the nickname 'Deadwood Dick' as champion of the West.

Some Blacks joined the US Army. Four segregated regiments were sent to fight in the lawless West where cattlemen fought farmers, Native Americans tried to keep Whites off their land and outlaws attacked everybody. Blacks won 14 Medals of Honor in the 'Indian' wars against the Native Americans.

Cooper

Anna Julia Cooper (1858–1964) went to one of the new schools for freed slaves after the Civil War. Later, at teachers' training college, she protested about the attitude to women. She became a teacher in Washington and then a headteacher. In 1925 she got her doctorate in Paris. She published a book, in French, about French attitudes to slavery. She returned to Washington to open a school for Black workers.

6.4 Black Struggles and Achievements

The situation was particularly difficult for Black women, who were rejected by White women and sometimes treated as inferior by Black men. In towns and cities some Black women formed their own organizations. They offered help to the poor and to newly arrived migrants. They raised money for schools, orphanages, teacher training colleges and old people's homes.

One of the most active women was **Ida B. Wells**. Born a slave, she became a crusading journalist on a Black newspaper in Memphis, Tennessee. When three young Black men were lynched in 1892 she wrote articles attacking the murders. Threatened, she fled to Chicago and began an international campaign against lynching. She became a leading member of several women's groups, including the **National Association of Colored Women**. Mary Mcleod Bethune became president of the Association in 1924.

Dr W. E. B. DuBois, a writer and sociologist, founded the **Niagara Movement** in 1905 to try to get Black people's legal rights restored. This movement had many supporters in both North and South.

Ida B. Wells, protesting to President McKinley about the lynching of a Black postmaster in 1898.

William Walling describing riots in 'The Independent', 1908.

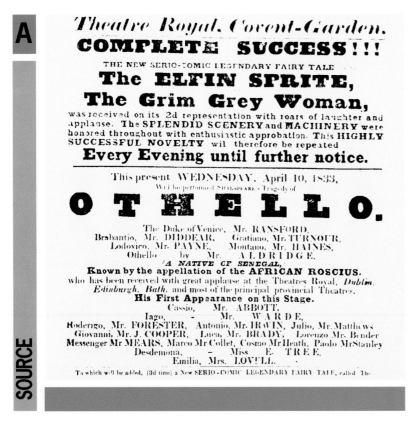

A playbill for Shakespeare's 'Othello' featuring Ira Aldridge, a leading African-American actor.

In 1908 there was a three day race riot in Springfield, Illinois. Three men were lynched. Some liberal White people, horrified by the violence, invited leading Blacks, including Ida B. Wells and Dr DuBois, to attend a meeting. A new group was formed called the **National Association for the Advancement of Colored People**. It was led by Whites but Dr DuBois was appointed as Director of Research and editor of its paper, *The Crisis*. The NAACP became the main organization fighting for Black people's rights in courts of law.

Dr George Washington Carver with students in his laboratory at Tuskegee, Alabama.

E

Dr Daniel Williams was the first surgeon in the world to perform a heart operation (1893).

Granville Woods invented an automatic air brake for trains.

Jan Matzeliger invented a machine that practically made an entire shoe in one operation (1883).

Madam C. J. Walker invented a hair conditioner and cosmetics for Black women, making herself a millionaire (1905).

Books were published by, among others, **Martin Delany** (1859), **Frances Harper** (1892), **Paul Lawrence Dunbar** (1898), **Frederick Douglass** (1845), **Harriet Jacobs** (1861).

Black musicians, singers and dancers began appearing in Broadway musicals from the turn of the century.

Dr George Washington Carver developed 350 uses for Southern agricultural products.

Some leading Black men and women during this time.

DuBois

Dr W. E. B. DuBois (1868–1963) was the first Black to get a doctorate from Harvard University. He became one of the most important leaders of Black protest in the USA. He was probably the first person to have the idea of **Pan-Africanism**, the belief that all people of African descent have common interests and should work together to end prejudice. DuBois was a historian and sociologist. He attended the first Pan-African Conference in London in 1900. He later organized such conferences in Europe and the USA.

DuBois opposed the idea that Blacks could better themselves through hard work because he thought that Blacks must speak out against discrimination. He said the way to end it was for educated Blacks to make their demands for justice heard. He worked with the Niagara Movement and NAACP but after 1948 he became more upset with how slowly race relations moved in the USA. He moved to Ghana, where he died.

7.1 The Americas and Africa

Smuggling slaves to the Americas ended with the freeing of the slaves in Brazil in 1888. But that was not the end of the link between Africa and the Americas.

A two-way traffic had developed. As we have seen, some Africans migrated to the West Indies. Others, especially from South Africa, were encouraged by missionaries to go to the USA to study.

Black people from North America immigrated to Liberia and Sierra Leone. Both these places in West Africa had been earmarked as homes for Blacks from the USA and Britain respectively. Martin Delany had visited Liberia and Nigeria, where he asked for land from the Yoruba kings. Freed Blacks from Brazil and the West Indies, including Cuba, also resettled in West Africa and the Congo River area.

Black American religious colleges trained missionaries to go to Africa. Many carried on the racist myths that Whites had held about Africa. They went to bring 'civilization' to the 'Dark Continent'. In 1884 the European countries which wanted to take more land in Africa met in Berlin to divide the whole continent, except Liberia and Ethiopia, between them.

In reply African-Americans held a meeting in Chicago in 1893. They supported immigration to Africa and condemned colonial ideas. In 1897, Henry Sylvester Williams, a Trinidadian lawyer who worked in London, formed the **African Association**. In 1900 the Association called the first **Pan-African Congress** which united Africans from all over the world. The US delegation was led by Dr DuBois. Black Britons who were there included the composer Samuel Taylor-Coleridge and J. R. Archer, who became Mayor of Battersea, London, in 1913.

A SOURCE

Those on the south of the River Niger, and near its mouths, are in the depths of savagery. This has been intensified by the slave-stealing and slave-dealing which we long encouraged in them, and by the trade in gin and rum, in guns and gunpowder, which we still zealously carry out with them.

R. H. Fox-Bourne, Secretary of the British Aborigines Protection Society, 1899.

'The main stream came up to Susi's mouth and wetted my seat and legs', David Livingstone, exploring Africa.

B SOURCE

In 1911 Dr DuBois was in London again at the Universal Races Congress. Also there was Dusé Mohamed Ali, an Egyptian who later started a newspaper. In 1913 a young Jamaican, **Marcus Garvey**, asked for a job on the newspaper. The following year, Garvey returned home to Jamaica. On August 1, Emancipation Day, he started the **Universal Negro Improvement Association**, which was to inspire Africans the world over by proclaiming the worth, talents and potential of Black peoples everywhere.

The Crest of Liberia.

1 To secure civil and political rights for Africans and their descendants throughout the world;

2 To encourage friendly relations between the Caucasian and African races;

3 To encourge African peoples everywhere in educational, industrial and commercial enterprise;

4 To approach Governments and influence legislation in the interests of the Black races; and

5 To ameliorate the condition of the oppressed Negro in Africa, America, the British Empire and other parts of the world.

The aims of the London based Pan-African Association, formed in 1900.

The problem of the twentieth century is the problem of the color-line, the question as to how far differences of race – which show themselves chiefly in the color of the skin and the texture of the hair – will hereafter be made the basis of denying to over half the world the right of sharing to their utmost ability the opportunity and privileges of modern civilization.

The proclamation addressed 'To the Nations of the World' written by W. E. B. DuBois at the 1900 Pan-African Congress held in London.

Garvey

Marcus Garvey (1887–1940) founded the Universal Negro Improvement Association in Jamaica in 1914. He took the Association to the USA in 1916. It offered new hope for Blacks who were upset by the anti-Black riots of 1918–19, racial discrimination and the lack of recognition of the part Blacks played in World War I. By the 1920s, Garvey had over two million followers in 38 states. He said that Blacks should be proud of their race and achievements and have hope and self respect.

He believed that Blacks would not receive justice in countries that were White-dominated. Garvey believed that all Blacks should settle in Africa, their homeland. He did much to encourage racial pride and a working class consciousness. Garvey financed his work with business ventures which ended as failures. In 1923 Garvey was jailed for fraud, but his conviction was questionable. He lost his former status and returned to Jamaica. He was driven out by opponents and died in London.